OPERA OMNIA
OR, A DUET FOR SITAR AND TROMBONE

LUXORIUS

Opera omnia

or, a DUET *for* SITAR *and* TROMBONE

Translated *from the Latin by* Art Beck

OTIS BOOKS | SEISMICITY EDITIONS
The Graduate Writing program
Otis College of Art and Design
LOS ANGELES ● 2012

Versions of some of these translations and material from the introduction and afterword have appeared in the journals *Alaska Quarterly Review, Artful Dodge, Invisible City, OR, Passages North, RE:AL, Sequoia, Translation Review, Tundra* and *Two Lines* and in the fine press limited editions *Simply to See* (Berkeley, Poltroon) and *Art Beck Translates Luxorius* (New York Book Arts)

Book design and typesetting: Rebecca Chamlee

ISBN-13: 978-0-9845289-6-7
ISBN-10: 0-9845289-5-4

OTIS BOOKS | SEISMICITY EDITIONS
The Graduate Writing program
Otis College of Art and Design
9045 Lincoln Boulevard
Los Angeles, CA 90045

http.gw.otis.edu
https://blogs.otis.edu/seismicity
seismicity@otis.edu

Table of Contents

Introduction: Conversations With the Dead

I. FINDING LUXORIUS

I first stumbled on Luxorius some thirty years ago. As is typical with ghostly visitations, the exact time that a small green volume slipped itself into my hand while wandering the old San Francisco main library stacks is elusive. It seems like yesterday. But, today, browsing old magazines, I notice I published a Luxorius translation in *Invisible City* in 1974. It may have been my first Luxorius translation. I can't really remember.

The volume in the no longer existent stacks was Morris Rosenblum's 1961 (Columbia University Press) *Luxorius: A Latin Poet Among the Vandals*. A publication that appears adapted from Rosenblum's doctoral thesis. There were two things that attracted me.

One was Luxorius' story: Not only an obscure poet, but a truly lost poet: Writing at the dawn of the dark ages, around 525 A.D., in Roman North Africa. A place that had been occupied by the German Vandals and cut off from Italy for a hundred years. But a vibrant and thriving place, paradoxically in large part because it was insulated from the disintegrating Western Empire. That false Eden came to an end during Luxorius' lifetime. In 534, the Byzantine Eastern Empire invaded the rich North African provinces and reclaimed what Rome and the West couldn't hold. It worked for a while, and then didn't. History and anarchy prevailed like a relentless storm, until finally Luxorius' ironic, quizzical, post-Classical world was swept into the new Medieval reality.

His poems are collected in only one manuscript. The *Anthologia Latina*: A compilation of fifteen contemporary North African poets laced with a broad sampling of Classical

Latin authors. The *Anthologia* appears to date from shortly after the restoration of Imperial rule. Luxorius has 91 poems in the *Anthologia*, more than any other poet.

Only one copy of the *Anthologia Latina* is known, and that copy remained unknown until it surfaced in France in 1615. Except for scattered, sometimes anonymous, poems in a few medieval manuscripts, *Luxorius was literally lost for a thousand years.*

Browsing the green volume, I had a sense that the lines in the short Latin poems in Rosenblum's thesis were somehow still living things, trapped in a scholar's web like wriggling specimens. And reading further, I found that something like this was indeed the case with the resurrected manuscript. The *Anthologia* and Luxorius' poems were preserved by copyist monks from a lost original. The monks not only copied the poems, but catalogued them with titles written in later, medieval Latin that in some cases had little to do with the entitled poem.

For these tonsured scholars, the culture Luxorius represented was gone, the world had changed, mankind was saved. One didn't throw antiquity and one's ancestors away, but the poems were artifacts of a bankrupt age, as irrelevant as childhood souvenirs. Most simply needed to be labeled and stored. *Especially those that were obscene.* There was no need for anyone but scholars to have access to Luxorius.

Even resurrected, Luxorius remains obscure. He's had few translators and has rarely been taken very seriously as a poet. Rosenblum claimed his thesis was the first (and still only) complete translation of Luxorius into any language. But the study seems more a historical than literary project and Rosenblum, as well, didn't seem overly impressed with Luxorius. Certainly nowhere nearly as impressed as the anonymous author of a short poem in the *Anthologia* who wrote:

> *Priscos, Luxuri, certum est te vincere vates:*
> > *Carmen namque tuum duplex Victoria gestat.*

It's certain you've surpassed
the ancient poets, Luxorius,
for surely your inspired poem is
swept aloft on a double victory.

II. THE OTHER ATTRACTION

All this was interesting, but beyond his story, what attracted me to
Luxorius was a certain tap on the shoulder as I read Rosenblum's
prose trots. A certain presence shaking its head. Whispering: *You
know, there's really more here than this theorizing professor wants
to see.* But not a whisper, because the spirits don't whisper. They
appear in absolute silence and maintain their silence. They simply
slip into your head.

The poem in the 1974 *Invisible City* is an example of how
Luxorius seemed to turn from words on paper into voice for me.
Here's the Latin and Dr. Rosenblum's prose translation:

De rustica in disco facta, quae spinam tollit de planta satyri

Cauta nimis spinam satyri pede rustica tollit,
*   Luminibus certis vulneris alta notans.*
Illum panduri solatur voce Cupido,
*   Intidens tali vulnere flere virum.*
Nil falsum credas artem luisse figuris:
*   Viva minus speciem reddere membra solent.*

*About a Country Girl Pictured on a Plate Removing a Thorn from
a Satyr's Foot.*

*A country girl is very carefully removing a thorn from a satyr's
foot, while peeping at the deep wound with great concern. Playing
a pandora (a musical instrument) Cupid is consoling him but
also mocks him because he, a man, is crying over such a wound.
You would believe that art has not given a single false touch to the
figures; living beings are usually less lifelike.*

There was a tone, an aesthetic, an accessibility, a seductiveniss in this poem that seemed to want to migrate to 1970s California. Since Rosenblum noted that the titles of Luxorius' poems were added later, I immediately shortened the title. And knowing no one would know what a "pandora" was without research, I changed the instrument first to a guitar, and then, for the sake of the image to a flute. And began tinkering. The result wasn't anything all that heavy, but it was the beginning of a dialogue with an elusive presence, my own "inner Luxorius."

Figures on a Plate

How cautiously the country girl lifts the thorn
out of the Satyr's foot. All the while clucking,
scolding the unquestionably horrible gash.
Cupid, dressed up like a flute player
stands there muttering his ridiculous consolations
...a grown man crying? Moaning over a little
cut like that?...
And where does art borrow to lend this
kind of life to the stock figures? Real
human beings are hardly this vital.

So I began to translate Luxorius – intermittently, the way one would visit a new friend, cautiously, so as not to wear out my welcome. *But I never hesitated to shamelessly indulge in what Professor Rosenblum so sternly warned against on the first page of his preface.* "There is need of reappraisal... because certain scholars have attempted to rewrite Luxorius according to their ideas of what they would have written if they had developed the themes of Luxorius' poems."

This was, after all the '70s, when what Rosenblum deplored seemed what poetic translation was all about: Dancing on the high wire that divides re-creation from appropriation. Some twenty years later, in a chapbook introduction, I characterized my Luxorius translations as "guesses, not statements." Not only because of the obscurity and possible corruption of some of the texts, but because... "at best, every translation contains an inter-jected voice, an unanticipated duet." In Luxorius' case, given the leaps over cultural chasms, I thought the translations might be described as "transcriptions from sitar to trombone."

What kept bringing me back to Luxorius was that duet, a sense of hidden conversation. Trying to translate, the Latin of course, but also the still somehow alive underlying poem that first found its expression in Latin, and now wanted to try English. A conjuring act? A ouija board, a foray into the occult? I browsed Luxorius in no particular order, stopping on images that caught my eye. And I took comfort in Luxorius' own haunted sense of history. Writing – knowingly or not – at the end of his civilization, he seemed to have little interest in the new, the Christian, the nascent medieval. But he took little solace from the Classical. The gods and myths seem to haunt – not console – him.

III. IMAGINING LUXORIUS

To converse with Luxorius, you have to visualize Roman North Africa. A fertile region then, originally colonized by Rome after the Punic wars, it developed, beginning with Augustus, into "the granary of the empire." Its large *latifundia* produced not only grains and cereals, but olive oil, grapes, figs and a variety of fruit. The area also became highly urbanized with a cultural sophisti-cation equal to any in the Empire. The city of Carthage was said to be second only to Rome in the Western Empire. Roman North Africa produced Apuleius, Tertullian and Augustine of Hippo. If you think of Rome as, say, New York, "Libya" might be California.

Then, in the early fifth century, the Vandals, a Germanic tribe, migrated from Spain to North Africa, gradually took control of the rich Roman provinces, and established the "Vandal Empire," holding North Africa for some hundred years. Unique among Rome's barbarian invaders, they'd become a viable naval power.

And with their fleet, they ensured that trade and North African prosperity continued. After a series of wars, Genseric the wily Vandal patriarch was able to negotiate uneasy truces with both the Western and Eastern Empires. In 455, Genseric took the opportunity to capture and loot the city of Rome after the Emperor Valentinian III was assassinated by a usurper. He left, after two weeks, considerably enriched, taking Valentian's widow and daughter with him back to Africa, where he married the dead emperor's daughter to one of his sons.

In picturing the 5th and 6th century Vandals, it's probably more accurate to conjure the image of Prince Valiant, rather than Atilla the Hun. The Vandals numbered less than a hundred thousand in a population of many millions, but formed a stable military ruling class during a period that coincided with the fall of the Western Roman Empire. Except for being "Arian heretics" and zealously persecuting orthodox Catholics, they enthusiastically adapted Roman ways. That the Vandals were engaged enough with the bishoprics and doctrines of the Christian establishment to be heretics might, in fact, be taken as a sign of their civilized status.

Latin remained the official language and the Roman legal, commercial and educational system continued undisturbed. Although the Vandals began issuing their own, low denomination coins in 477, high denomination coinage remained Imperial. The Vandals seem as much immigrants as rulers. They came to North Africa to live like Romans: To be as Roman as the Romans. The land was worthless without the civilization. The Empire officially considered the Vandals pirates and usurpers. But North Africa had been violently torn by chronic religious and social unrest for a generation. The West was steadily disintegrating. For most North African Romans, the blond barbarians seem to have represented not a "yellow peril," but – "a kind of solution."

For Luxorius, the Vandals seem simply to be "the establishment." There's no particular sense that Carthage was an occupied territory. The Vandals seem "different," not in their foreignness, but in the sense that "the very rich are different from you and me." Although Luxorius' attitude seems closer to Hemingway's "yeah, they have more money," than Fitzgerald's awe.

Luxorius' poems deal with a variety of subjects; with high and low life. Pimps and lawyers, blood sport athletes, chariot racers, finance ministers, grammarians, prisoners, priests and Vandal royalty are seen though a single set of eyes and dissected in a singular voice. His vision – like that of the venator with eyes painted on his hands, or the blind man in the brothel – is almost tactile. For me his voice seems sinuous, never raised. He's a *poeta*, not a *vatens*. He speaks, not as an oracle, but in the reader's own intimate voice. But though he's not speaking for the ages, he somehow preserves his age and conveys a surprisingly immediate sense of a powerful urban heartbeat; the chaos and fecundity of a big, old city. A culture that's been around and has seen it all, but still wants to see more.

IV: THE FLOWERING GODDESS

In his study, Morris Rosenblum revives a 19th century controversy among German classicists over Luxorius' possible Christianity. That question, rightly significant to the classicists who asked it because religion was such an important dynamic of Late Antiquity, probably wouldn't occur to a casual 21st century reader. Christian solace is notably absent from Luxorius' work. His few references to Christian beliefs and practices are ironic, at best. Striking pagan images abound, but these also seem to lack religious conviction. For Luxorius, who lived in a society saturated with religious fanaticism and warring Christian sects, religious belief of any kind doesn't seem viable.

With, possibly, the exception of the goddess Venus. Who, in one poem, *somehow still lives*. In another, she returns to inhabit and infuse her marble statue. Similar to Apollo's ripening "eye-apples" in Rilke's *Archaic Torso*, Luxorius imagines Venus pouring *her own special heat / into every part of the statue until / it comes alive with flowers / No need to lie about where: / A violet doorway whose delicacy's / guarded by a swell of handmaiden roses.*

And Venus is also incarnate in the *Centofilia,* the *hundred-petal rose… permeated with all of Venus' pulsing blood… the proud flower, gracious morning star of the meadow. Its fragrance, its blush, merit heaven's respect.*

It's in that implicit elevation of the erotic to the sacred that I think Luxorius may be unique among Latin epigrammatists. He's often referred to as the "North African Martial." Probably a quarter of Luxorius' poems deal with sex, most quite blatantly. Whatever the reception in Luxorius' time, his (mostly nineteenth century) scholarly reputation is generally as a poet of crudity and decadence. Following this tradition, Roseblum references poems under subject headings such as "poems about amatory defectives" and "poems about perverts."

One man's liberation is another's decadence and it's pointless to argue morality at this cultural distance. But, I think the crudity is a bum rap. Martial, for one, has an obsession with sexual mockery and seldom takes a poem beyond the dirty joke or epithet. Luxorius' situations are more finely drawn, more evocative: Some, quite explicitly, some more covertly. Sometimes satiric and sometimes sympathetic, but always at a high level of psychological sophistication. Homophobic mockery is a stock subject of the Latin epigram. But Luxorius' homophobic forays seem to contain a chord-like echo of homoeroticism, an empathy beneath the banter.

Conversely for Martial, roses and genitalia are not a synapse. And Luxorius' gentle evocation of the restorative powers of oral sex in his allegory of the she-bear, who *licks things into shape / first with her uterus, and then / with her wise tongue,* would probably be lost on Martial who cringes at being kissed by all the "cocksuckers and cuntlappers" in the teeming Roman streets.

V. THE THOUSAND-YEAR SLEEP

Vandal rule came to a sudden end during Luxorius' lifetime when Justinian's general Belisarius invaded and re-claimed North Africa for the Eastern Empire. But the restoration of Roman rule was abortive. After most of the Vandal nobility was killed or sold into slavery, Belisarius was recalled to Constantinople leaving only a small core contingent of troops. The provinces couldn't be ruled from Constantinople. Mutinies, populist insurrections, terrorism, religious and guerrilla warfare followed the Byzantine Roman overthrow of Vandal "tyranny." The contemporary Byzantine historian Procopius – who may or may not be accurate – *but who was there*, says that some five million people died directly or indirectly as a result of the "Vandallic War." And laments that "Libya," once so prosperous and populous, was "now a wasteland."

The remnants of the Greek-speaking Byzantine army that "liberated" Roman Africa were reduced to taking stones from Roman monuments to build fortresses against Berber uprisings, marauding Bedouins and renegade Roman military units. Little by little, Provincial government crumbled, and commerce was crippled as cities and towns became isolated strongholds. Fertile farmland slowly reverted to wilderness.

Finally, late in the 7th century, after stubborn resistance, Carthage fell again – this time to the Arab Muslims. Africa, "three days sail from Rome," became Ifriqaya. The Latin language faded and disappeared.

Who knows whether the fifteen African poets of the *Anthologia Latina* – Avitus, Bonusus, Calbulus, Caro, Coronatus, Flavius Felix, Florentinus, Lindinus, Luxorius, Modestinus, Octavianus, Ponnanus, Regianus, Tuccianus, Vincentius – sensed the destruction to come? Their *Anthology*, interestingly, along with the Vandal Empire poets, includes a broad sampling of Classical Roman works – selections from Virgil, Ovid, Propertius, Seneca, and Martial among others.

Like everything connected with the fall of the Roman Empire, the *Anthologia Latina* has engendered its share of imaginative scholarly speculation. So perhaps one more fantasy might be forgiven. Isn't it remotely possible that the North African poets, considering their fragile uneasy world, might have wanted to construct a time capsule for themselves and so protected their manuscripts with venerated ancients they hoped conscientious monkish archivists would preserve? That Faustus, the veteran editor, conscripted those long dead poets from a lost Empire to serve as lead soldiers guarding the cargo of a paper boat consigned to a stormy gutter? Who knows? Like Luxorius' blind man in the brothel, we sniff, grope, feel something real – and imagine as best we can.

Caveat Lector

Although a "complete" Luxorius, these are interpretive translations and not intended as authoritative, i.e. my purpose was aesthetic, not scholarly.

Indeed, the "authority" of segments of the Latin text itself might be questioned, in that it exists in only one extant copy compiled centuries after the original. It contains quizzical spellings, usages and lacunae variously emended by a small group of scholars, who largely seemed to view the material as having historical, but only marginal poetic, value.

The poetic advantage of a "collected" rather than "selected" Luxorius is that it accesses as broad a range as possible to explore the nuances of a sometimes elusive and tenuous voice. The Latin is provided as a touchstone of breath and sound, and – for those with some fluency – an invitation to explore other possibilities and their own duet.

A Note on the Latin Titles

The titles in the *Codex* manuscript have been questioned by most scholars and it's considered doubtful that any of Luxorius' titles are authentic. Rosenblum points out that many contain Latin usage that post dates Luxorius and read like obvious catalog headings appended by a much later compiler. Most importantly, a number of the Latin titles clash with the sense of the poems or flatten, impede and ignore essential paradoxes in an attempt to summarize. Some of the more descriptive titles even interject images or interpretations extraneous to the poem. It seems reasonable to presume that Luxorius' poems, like Martial's, Horace's, Catullus', et al, were probably untitled.

Titles, however, can be a useful tool for an interpreter as well as a compiler. I preferred to disregard all the Latin titles, but in some cases to use a made up title to clarify what might be obvious in Latin but obscure in English. In other cases, I simply used the poem's first line as a title. In poems 26, 38, 70, 79 and 88, my reading contradicts the Latin titles.

Metro Phalaecio ad Faustum

Ausus post veteres, tuis, amice,
Etsi iam temere est, placere iussis,
Nostro Fauste animo probate conpar,
Tantus grammaticae magister artis,
Quos olim puer in foro paravi
Versus ex variis locis deductos
(Illos scilicet unde me poetam
Insulsum puto quam magis legendum),
Nostri temporis ut amavit aetas,
In parvum tibi conditos libellum
Transmisi memori tuo probandos
Primum pectore; deinde, si libebit,
Discretos titulis quibus tenentur,
Per nostri similes dato sodales,
Nam, si doctiloquis nimisque magnis
Haec tu credideris viris legenda,
Culpae nos socios notabit index –
Tam te, talia qui bonis recenses,
Quam me, qui tua duriora iussa
Feci nescius, immemor futuri.
Nec me paeniteat iocos secutum
Quos verbis epigrammatom facetis
Diversos facili pudore lusit
Frigens ingenium, laboris expers.
Causam, carminis unde sit voluptas,
Edet ridiculum sequens poema.

I

Like an audacious old veteran after it's

over, dear friend – even though it really is
risky now – but to please you since you asked –
and because I want to be recognized as a kindred spirit
of our great master of arts and letters, Faustus, I've
trotted out these verses from various places.
Some of them date from my school
days in the forum, and they're as tasteless
as you'd expect from a beginner who thought
he was a poet. But our generation loved these trifles
in its time, and I've kept them in the volume
and pass them on to you to remember.
Pass judgement on all of them with your generous heart.
Take what pleases you, re-arrange them in whatever
order or sections you like. Then hand them around
to our little fraternity.

And, if you're still insistent on their
being read by finer, more eloquent voices,
we'll both be pointed at as equal partners in disgrace.
You, for believing such things have any place
among the good. Me, for adhering to your stern
ascetic – blindly, without a thought of my future.
But I don't repent following that path
of least resistance. The dirty words in my epigrams.
The unpretentious play of my jokes.
My talent's frigid reception.
The absence of shame in my work:
They're the reasons my songs are seductive and
why you're publishing this absurd collection of poems.

II

Iambici ad lectorem operis suis

Prisocs cum haberes quos probares indices,
Lector, placere qui bonis possent modis,
Nostri libelli cur retrexis paginam
Nugis refertam frivolisque sensibus,
Et quam tenello tiro lusi viscere?
An forte doctis illa cara est versibus,
Sonat pusillo quae laboris schemate,
Nullo decoris, ambitus, sententiae?
Hanc tu requiris et libenture inchoas,
Velut iocosa si theatra pervoles.

2

You have the acceptable old titles

to please you with their fine
modalities. Why bother to unravel
the pages of this book of mine
that's crammed with trivialities
and empty attitudes all the way to its dainty
innards of naive delusion?
Maybe, by chance, you treasure
being instructed by verses
which say hardly anything in a labored
style, avoiding elegance, subtlety,
meaning? Actually, you need to get
hold of and begin this little book
as if you were flitting off
to a theatre of jokes.

III

Asclepiadei ad librum suum

Parvus nobilium cum liber ad domos
Pomoposique fori scrinia publica
Cinctus multifido veneris agmine,
Nostri defugiens pauperia laris,
Quo dudum modico sordidus angulo
Squalebas, tineis iam prope deditus,
Si te despiciet turba legentium
Inter Romulidas et Tyrias manus,
Isto pro exequiis claudere disticho:
"Contentos propriis esse decet focis
Quos laudis facile est invidiam pati."

3

Little volume when you're delivered

to the homes of the nobles and are enshrined
in the public stacks of the library in the forum,
to be taken up by the multitude; you'll have
finally escaped our impoverished household
where for years you hid, mourning in a squalid
corner, nearly abandoned to bookworms.
And, if the restless Roman and African literary
crowd tears you apart, close with two last lines:
"Stay home at peace where you belong for as long
as you can possibly endure your jealousy of praise."

IV

Epigrammata parva quod in hoc libros scripserit

....
    Si quis hoc nostro detrahit ingenio,
Adtendat modicis condi de mensibus annum,
    Et graciles hiemis, veris et esse dies;
Noverit in brevibus magnum deprendier usum.
    Ultra mensuram gratia nulla datur.
Sic mea concinno si pagina displicet actu,
    Finito citius carmine clausa silet.
Nam, si constaret libris longissima multis,
    Fastidita forent plurima vel vitia.

4

On Short Poems

....
whoever disparages my talent because of this should
remember that spring and all the months of the year
rest on a foundation of simple, unadorned winter days.
And remember the sayings: Great things are usually
an accumulation of the small. Excess never gains favor.
Supposing my compact pages take an offensive turn,
the poem will get where it's going quickly
and be silent. Because, the longer the book, the more
pretentious, the more faults to reveal.

V

Trochaicum de piscibus qui ab hominibus cibos capiebant

Verna clausas inter undas et lacunas regias
Postulat cibos diurnos ore piscis parvolo
Nec manum fugit vocatus nec pavescit retia.
Roscidi sed amnis errans hinc et inde margine,
Odit ardui procellas et dolosi gurgitis,
Ac suum quo libet esse transnatans colit mare.
Sic fames gestu loquaci et mitiori vertice
Discit ille quam sit aptum ventris arte vincere.

5

Fish

A pampered house pet, confined among the waves
of the royal pool, presents itself to claim its daily
ration of nourishment with its little fish mouth.
When summoned, it doesn't run from the hand, isn't
frightened of any nets, but, in fact, wanders back and forth
along the egde as if keeping to the shallows of a river.
It's as terrified of the deep end as of a treacherous
whirlpool. It's happy to swim in its own
appropriate sea. And with the lip-smacking gestures
and gentle head bobs its empty belly's taught it,
shows how easy it is to conquer hunger.

VI

Archilochium de apro mitissimo in triclinio nutrito

Martis aper genitus iugus inesse montium
Frangere et horrisonum nemus ferocius solens,
Pabula porticibus capir libenter aureis
Et posito famulans furore temperat minas.
Nec Parios lapides revellit ore spumeo
Atria nec rabidis decora foedat ungulis
Sed domini placidam manum quietus appetens
Fit magis ut Veneris dicatus ille sit sacris.

6

A wild boar—an animal of Mars, born

to roam the high mountains when it's not ferociously
invading and terrorizing the sacred groves –
now tamed – takes its nourishment in gilded galleries
and, like a faithful servant, calmly controls his
aggressive nature. He doesn't tear up the splendid
marble with his foaming tusks or mar the delicate
mosaics with his rabid hoofs, just gently licks his master's
calm hands: A creature who ought to be consecrated
to Venus, not sacrificed to Mars.

VII

De auriga Aegyptio qui semper vincebat

Quamvis ab Aurora fuerit genetrice creatus
    Memnon, Pelidae conruit ille manu.
At te Nocte satum, ni fallor, matre paravit
    Aeolus et Zephyri es natus in antra puer.
Nec quisquam qui te superet nascetur Achilles.
    Dum Memnon facie es, non tamen es genio.

7

The Charioteer They Call "Memnon"

King Memnon's mother, the Dawn herself, gave
him life: Peleus' son broke him in his two hands.

But, if I'm not mistaken, your mother was Night
and she slipped off with Aeolus to the cave

of the West Wind to plant you. So, it's not
as if another Achilles will have to be born

to beat you. You may be black
like Memnon, but you're not related.

VIII

Sapphicum in grammaticum furiosum

Carminum interpres meritique vatum,
Cum leves artem pueros docere
Diceris vel te iuvenes magistrum
Audiunt verbis veluti disertum
Cur in horrendam furiam recedis
Et manu et telo raperis cruentus?
Non es, in quantum furor hic probatur,
Dignus inter grammaticos vocari
Sed malos inter sociari Orestas.

8

Critical Interpreter of Lyrics and Epics

You instruct little boys in the rudiments
and lead discussions among the adolescents,
who hang on your eloquent words, your
masterful gestures – especially when you draw
back in horrified shock as if your hands
held a bloodstained weapon? Doesn't this
very fury just reveal you're not respectable
enough to be a grammarian and teach
the mother tongue; that you really are more
comfortable with villains like Orestes.

IX

Glyconeum in advocatum effiminatem

Exceti species viri.
Naturae grave dedecus,
Usu femineo Paris,
Foeda cura libidinis,
Cum sis ore facundior,
Cur causus steriles agis
Aut corrupta negotia
Et perdenda magis locas?
Agnovi. Ut video, tuo
Ori quid bene credier
Non vis sed, puto, podici.

9

Opposing Counsel

The very image of a cute eunuch, a serious
disgrace to nature. Submissive, languorous,
feminine. "Make a date" and you "promise
you'll take special care to satisfy..."

You have such a persuasive mouth,
why is it you only seem to plead
fruitless cases, sleazy deals,
accept such unwinnable assignments?

It's coming to me. I see why now.
You don't trust yourself not to gag
on anything too strong, you'd rather
argue those cases with your asshole.

In clamosum Pygmaeum corpore et furiosum

Corpore par querulis es vel clamore cicadis –
    Hinc potior quod te tempora nulla vetant.
Dum loqueris, quaerunt cuncti vox cuius oberret,
    Atque sonum alterius corporis esse putant.
Miramur, tantum capiant qui membra furorem,
    Cum sit forma levis, clamor et ira gravis.

Pygmy

Your body's even shaped like a clamoring cricket's –
although your complaints aren't limited to any particular season.
When you speak, everyone asks whose voice
is reverberating. They can't believe it's not coming from
another body. I wonder how your limbs can contain so much fury.
Such a silly little form, bellowing with the weight of its rage.

*Phalaecium in moechum quod debriatus plorabat cum
coitum inplere non posset*

Saepius futuis nimisque semper,
Nec parcis, nisi forte debriatus
Effundis lacrimas qho esse moechus
Multo non valeas mero subactus.
Plura ne futuas, peto, Lucine,
Aut semper bibe taediumque plange,
Aut, numquam ut futuas, venena sume.

II

As if almost by chance, but all too often now – and always

when you're really wild to fuck – your drinking reins
you in and you shed the bitter tears of a not
good for much philanderer tamed by pure, unadulterated
wine. If you want more fucking, Lucinus – either just keep on
drinking and moaning – or quit fucking yourself with the poison.

XII

In spadonem regium qui mitellam sumebat

Rutilo decens capillo
Roseoque crine ephebus
Spado regius mitellam
Capiti suo locavit.
Proprii memor pudoris.
Bene conscius quid esset,
Posuit, cogente nullo,
Fuerat minus quod illi.

12

The pretty, red-headed, royal eunuch

sets a girl's bonnet on his unfurled rosy locks:
the boy's discreetly saying, he'd be glad –
no need to force him – to
slip out of his clothes for a little sail,
carried away by what he lacks.

XIII

Anapaesticum in magum mendicum

Tibi cum non sit diei panis,
Magicas artes inscius inples.
Ire per umbras atque sepulcra
Pectore egeno titubans gestis.
Nec tua Manes carmina summunt,
Fame dum pulsus Tartara cantu
Omnia turbas, aliquid credens
Dare quod possit superis Pluton
Pauperibus. Qui puto quod peius
Egeas totum semper in orbem,
Mage, si posces membra perempta.

13

Magus

You can't earn a steady living, so,
in your ignorance, you take up the magical
arts and ply your trade among shadows and graves,
your restless heart stammering, with deprivation
and need. But the spirits don't buy your song:
you disturb and repel the underworld
with your greedy, starved incantations, your
frustrating trust that Pluto is, somehow, capable
of returning anything to the destitute above.
Somehow, I suspect, magus, you'll always be worse
off than they are – anywhere you wander in this world
– if you beg from the dead.

In acceptorarium obesum et infelicem

Pondere detracto miseres, Martine, fatigas
Pressura crudelis aves. Pinguedine tanta
Ut tu sis, frustra maciem patiuntur iniquam.
Debuerant, fateor, magis has tua pascere membra,
Ut numquam posset ieiunia morte perire.

14

Falconer

You're obssessed with forcing down
the weight of your miserable birds, Martinus,
even while they relentlessy weaken.
And blubbery as you are, what purpose
does it serve for them to always be so gaunt
and desperate? If you'd acknowledged
your responsibility and fed them even
the scraps of what they brought you,
they'd never have starved to death.

In vetulam virginem nubentem

Virgo, quam Phlegethon vocat sororem,
Saturni potior parens senecta,
Quam Nox atque Erebus tulit Chaosque,
Cui rugae totidem graves quot anni,
Cui vultus elephans dedit cutemque,
Mater simia quam creavit arvis
Grandaeva in Lybicis novo sub orbe,
Olim quae decuit marita Diti
Pro nata Cereris dafri per umbras –
Quis te tam petulans suburit ardor,
Nunc cum iam exitium tibu supersit?
An hoc pro titulo cupis sepulcri,
Ut te cognita fama sic loquatur,
Quod stuprata viro est anus nocenti?

The Blushing Bride:

Whom the River Styx calls sister. Who's old enough
to be Saturn's ancestor. Whom night and Erebus
and primal Chaos brought forth. Whose

wrinkles are as many and as miserable as her
years. Whose complexion resembles an elephant's –
except your mother was probably a monkey

who dropped you in the Libyan desert,
long ago when the world was new. Who,
once upon a time, should have married Pluto,

so poor Ceres wouldn't have had to give her daughter
to the underworld. Why are you suddenly smoldering
with such impetuous heat? Just now, when all that's really

left for you in life is death? Is it that you long for
a fine inscription on your tomb, so you'll
be known and famous and talked about:

"Here lies an old woman, convicted of raping a man"?

In medicolenonem

Quod te pallidulum, Marine noster,
Cuncti post totidem dies salutant,
Credebam medicum velut peritum
Curam febribus et manum pudicam
De pactis logicae parare sectae
Aut de methodicis probare libris.
At tu fornice turpius vacabas,
Exercens aliis quod ipse possis
Lenatis melius tibi puellis
Scortandi solito labore ferre.
Novi quid libeat tuum chirurge,
Conspectos animum videre cunnos.
Vis ostendere te minus virum esse:
Arrectos satis est mares videre.

You looked so pale, my dear Marinus

when everyone welcomed you back after so many days
away. I thought – like the distinguished physician
you are – you must have been in the countryside curing
    fevers; then
preparing medical lectures for your dedicated apprentices;
and, in whatever spare time you could find, approving treatises
for publication. But, rather than tending to your practice,
    you were

having a dirty little vacation, running the brothel for the procurer.
Something you say you're suited for, not because you're a habitue',
but because you've treated the girls for so long. And now, I
remember how you used to love to demonstrate to us
that – given your lofty soul – inspecting a cunt had absolutely
no effect on you: Is it satisfaction enough
to see other men's erections?

In diaconum festinantem ad prandium cauponis

Quo festinus abis, gula inpellente, sacerdos?
   An tibi pro psalmis pocula corde sedent?
Pulpita templorum, ne pulpita quaere tabernae,
   Numina quo caeli, no phialas referas.

Is your parched gullet calling, Father?

You're in such a nervous hurry –
where is it you'd rather be?
While you soulfully intone the psalms,
your heart's really praying
for a cup, or two, or three of lovely wine.
Keep your mind on tabernacles,
Father, not taverns. It's almighty heaven
you're supposed to answer to, not the bottle.

*De turre in viridario posita, ubi se Fridamal aprum
pinxit occidere*

Extollit celsas nemoralis Aricia sedes,
    Sternit ubi famulas casta Diana feras.
Frondosis Tempe cinguntur Thessala silvis
    Pinguiaque Nemeae lustra Molorchus habet.
Haec vero aetherias exit quae turris in auras,
    Consessum domino deliciosa parans,
Omnibus in medium lucris ornata refulget
    Obtinuitque uno praemia cuncta loco.
Hinc nemus, hinc fontes extructa cubilia cingunt
    Statque velut propriis ipsa Diana iugis.
Clausa sed in tanto cum sit splendore voluptas
    Artibus ac variis atria pulcra micent,
Admiranda tuae tamen est virtutis imago,
    Fridamal, et stratae gloria magna ferae,
Qui solitae accendens mentem virtutis amore
    Aptasti digno pingere facta loco.
Hic spumantis apri iaculo post terga retorto
    Frontem et cum geminis naribus ora feris.
Ante ictum subita prostrata est bellua morte,
    Cui prius extingui quam cecidisse fuit.
Iussit fata manus telo, nec vulnera sensit
    Exerrans anima iam pereunte cruor.

Fridamal's Hunting Lodge

Sylvan Aricia exalts in its heavenly forests where
chaste Diana governs her animal brood.
Tempe, in Thessaly, is crowned with broad-leafed
woods, and Molorchus owns the rich Nemean wilderness.

Yet truly, Lord Fridamal has departed the earth
like a breeze for this ethereal mansion, this delightful
retreat, right here in the middle of everything glittering
money can buy – as great a prize as the sum
of all those other places combined.

The bedroom windows open on a fountained
grove that encircles its own Diana – as lifelike
as if she were striding the ridge-tops.
But it's indoors that the true pleasures

of art are found: The walls as magnificent as
a gallery and everything leading to the atrium
where our hero, Fridamal, as eager as any lover
to show off his manhood, has had himself –
and his worthy deed – captured in a painting
of the glorious overthrow of the great wild boar.

Standing there, calmly – javelin poised behind
his shoulder – aimed right between the flaring
nostrils of the foaming-mouthed face.
But before even being touched, the brute
has stumbled down lifeless at Fridamal's feet.
Commanded by the hand that wields the spear
to relinquish its soul to the moment of death,
without pain, anguish or bloodshed.

De avibus marinis quae post volatum ad domum remeabant

Felix marinis altibus Fridamal,
Felix iuventa, prosperior genio,
Quem sponte poscunt aequoreae volucres.
Nec stagna grato frigida concilio
Pigris strepentes gurgitibus retinent,
Sed quo tuoroum temperiem nemorum
Monstrent, volatu praememores famulo
Pro te relictam non repetunt patriam.

You're at peace with sea-birds, Fridamal;

content to be young; secure in the prosperous
destiny that seems to call to the aquatic wanderers.
Neither the quiet lagoons, nor the frigid, slow
gathering tides, nor the roaring undertow
can keep them from escaping
to your enchanting balmy groves –
where they flock like a proud household.
Because you're the reason – it's for you
they've forsaken and forgotten their ancestral home.

XX

In aurigam senem victum crimina in populos iactentem

Te quotiens victum circus, Cyriace, resultat,
    Crimine victores polluis et populos.
Non visum quereris senio languente perisse
    Castigasque tuae tarda flagella manus.
Sed quod in alterius divulgas crimina nomen,
    Cur non illa magis credis inesse tibi?
Es meritis inpar, virtute, aetate relictus.
    Haec cum habeant alii, crimina vera putas.
Sola tamen falsis surgat tibi poena loquellis,
    Ut victus semper nil nisi crimen agas.

Cyriacus

And when the race track reverberates with your defeat,
Cyriacus, you're always right there shouting at the winner
and at the crowd that you've been fouled. You never
think to fault your weak old eyes, or castigate your hesitating
whip hand. What makes you think you're exempt
from the deviousness you see in everyone else?
You're a relic of better days who doesn't have what it takes
to compete anymore – and when someone else does,
it's obvious you've been cheated. But the one verdict
that springs from all your deluded protests
is that you're not just a perpetual victim,
but the constant perpetrator of the crime.

In podagrum venationi studentem

Apros et capreas levesque cervos
Incurvus rapidis equis fatigat.
Tantum nec secquitur capitque quicquam.
Esse inter iuvenes cupit, vocari
Baudus, dum misero gemat dolore
Et nil praevaleat. Quid ergo gestit?
Mori praecipiti furit caballo,
Cum lecto melius perire possit.

Incurvus, on his quick horse, chases

boars, wild goats and little deer. He likes to always
hunt with the young men, likes to have them call him chief.
But he never seems to catch anything, and he's always groaning
about his pitiful aches and pains for which there are
no remedies, and he keeps throwing his hands in the air.
He's dying from being bounced by a galloping
stallion, when he might just as well die in bed.

In supra scriptum, quod multa scorta habuit et eas custodiebat

Zelo agitas plures, Incurvus, clune puellas,
    Sed nulla est quae te sentiat esse virum.
Custodis clausas, tamquam sis omnibus aptus.
    Est tamen internus Iuppiter ex famulis.
Si nihil ergo vales, vanum cur arrigis inguen
    Et facis ignavus mentis adulterium?

You're awfully jealous of all your girls' soft bottoms.

Incurvus (although none of them thinks
you're much of a man). And you keep them
under tight lock and key, as if you were capable
of doing the job on all of them, together.

But, then there's that other household slave of yours
– a regular Jupiter. Listen, whatever the reason your power
simply fails you, becomes such an empty yearning,
there's really no need to just lust in your heart.

Anacreaontium in medicum inpotentem qui ter viudal duxit uxorem.

Post tot repleta busta
Et funerum catervas
Ac dispares martos,
Rugosa quos peremit
Fatis anus sinistris,
Tu nunc, chirurge, quartus
Coniunx vocate plaudis.
Sed vivus es sepultus,
Dum parte qua decebat
Nil contines mariti.
Iam nosco: cui videtur
Nupsisse Paula rursus?
Nulli! Quid ergo fecit?
Mutare mox lugubrem
Quam sumpserat cupivit
Uxor nefanda vestem.
Ut quartus atque – quintus
Possit venire coniunx.

23

After the sumptuous, crowded funerals,

and after so many graves have been sated
with the unlucky husbands who weren't
equal to this wrinkled old woman

who was fated to kill them all: Now you,
Doctor, are proud to be be called
bridegroom number four.

And even though you're still breathing,
you're as good as buried.
Because you lack the equipment

that's needed to hold this marriage
together. Let me ask you: Who
do you really think Paula

wants to be married to, just now?
No one. And why is she doing this?
Could it be she's just restlesss to get

out of the mourning clothes
she so much wanted to change into
when she was still a cheating wife?

Just anxious to get back to normal life,
hopeful that – not her fourth – but
her fifth husband might soon come along?

*In pantomimam Pygmaem quae Andromachae fabulam
frequenter saltabat et raptum Helenae*

Andromacham atque Helenam saltat Macedonia semper
 Et quibus excelso corpore forma fuit.
Haec tamen aut brevior Pygmae virgine surgit
 Ipsius aut quantum pes erat Andromache.
Sed putat illarum fieri se nomine talem,
 Motibus et falsis crescere membra cupit.
Hac spe, crede, tuos incassum decipis artus.
 Thersiten potius fingem quod esse soles!

In the Trojan War Pantomimes,

Macedonia always dances Helen
and Andromache and the other tall,
stately, beauties. Even though she's
shorter than a Pygmy maiden and stands
just about as high as Andromache's foot.
She imagines as she dances and feels
her body stretch with hopeful longing.
But, hope, believe me, is just another insulting
lie to the body that was born for the role
of the ugly little Thersities, you really are.

In ebriosum nihil comedentem sed solum bibentem

Dum bibis solus pateras quot omnes,
Saepe nec totis satiaris horis
Et tibi munus Cereris resordet
Ac nihil curas nisi ferre Baccum,
Nerfa, iam te non hominem vocabo,
Sed nimis plenam et patulam lagonam.

Nerfa

While you drink as many cups
yourself as the rest of us together,
you rarely say you've had enough
no matter what the hour.
And though you make a spectacle
of the way you gobble, you're only
interested in breaking bread
as an accompaniment to wine.
Nerfa, you're no longer human,
just a wide mouth flagon
filled to the brim.

De Fama picta in stabulo circi

Qualem te pictor stabulis formavit equorum,
    Talem te nostris blanda referto iugis.
Semper et adsiduo vincendi munera porta
    His quorum limen fortis amica sedes.

Victory

The way the painter painted you on the stables –
just that same way – repay our team with caresses.
Make us consistent winners, and always remain
our formidable girlfriend at the gate.

Aliter

Verum Fama, tibi vultum pictura notavit,
    Daum vivos oculos iunceas forma gerit.
Tu, quamvis totum velox rapiaris in orbem,
    Pulcrior hoc uno limine clausa sedes.

27

Well, Fame, the painting is

a fine likeness, don't you think?
It really catches the life in your eyes
and your trim figure. With all that energy,
no wonder you're able to flit all over the world
so quickly. But you're so much more beautiful,
sitting down in one place, with the door closed.

In vicinum invidum

Zeleris nimium cur mea, Marcie,
Tamquan si pereas, limina, nescio,
Cum sis proximior, una velet domus,
Et nostros paries dimidiet lares.
Sed gratum ferimus. Talis et omnibus,
Nec quemquam nisi te vis miser aspici.
Contingat – quesumus, numina, – quod cupis!
Te solum ut videas, Marcie, dum visis.

Spite

Why this compulsive rivalry Marcius? We both
live in the same ruined neighborhood; next door, if you
please; one home, as it were – share the same *lares*
like a common wall. I don't take it personally:
You're the same with everyone, with any other
poor wretch but you who might command recognition.
May it happen – praise gods – that you get what you want
and have only yourself to recognize, Marcius, as long as you live.

In gibberosum qui se generosun iactabat

Fingis superbum quod tibi patrum genus,
Nunc Iuliorum prole et satum tumens,
Nunc Memmiorum Martiique Romuli,
Prodesse gibbo forte quid putas tuo?
Nil ista falso verba prosunt ambitu.
Tace parentes, ne quietos moveas.
Natura nobis unde sis natus docet.

Hunchback

Are you convinced it compensates for your
hump to trump up such a snobby lineage?
Now, you're descended from the haughty Julians,
except sometimes the Memmii get mixed in,
as well as Romulus, the son of Mars... Strutting
and lying isn't going to help it. Keep quiet
about your ancestors unless you want to
enrage the dead. It's obvious
what litter you're from.

De eo qui se poetam dicebat quod in triviis cantaret et a pueris laudaretur

Conponis fatuis dum pueris melos,
Zenobi, et trivio carmine perstrepis,
Indoctaque malis verba facis locis,
Credis tete aliquid laudibus indere
Famamque ad teneros ducere posteros?
Hoc nostrae faciunt semper et alites,
Ni rite instituis, sibila tum canunt.

Zenobius, when you write those slangy, stuttering poems

you call street songs and shout them in the neighborhood
taverns to the boorish boys, do you really think you're
establishing your reputation as a leader of the next generation?
Interesting, how – in all of us, without exception –
the untrained voice just hisses when it tries to really sing.

In puellam hermaphroditum

Monstrum feminei bimembre sexus,
Quam coacta virum facit libido,
Quin gaudes futui furente cunno?
Cur te decipit inpotens voluptas?
Non das, quo pateris facisque, cunnum.
Illam, qua mulier probaris esse,
Partem cum dederis, puella tunc sis.

Hermaphrodite Girl

As if you were a double-organed
monsterwoman who, rather than joyfully
stuffing herself
when she gets excited,
can't help her compulsive erection.

Why do you hide behind that frantic
pretend pleasure? You never really
give your cunt, neither open up nor squeeze.
If you want to prove you're a grown up woman,
quit playing the role and be my girl.

Ad eum qui per diem dormiens nocte vigilabat

Stertis anhelanti fessus quod corde, Lycaon,
    Exhorrens luci munera parta die,
Et tibi vigilias semper nos tetra minstrat,
    Iam scio te nostro vivere nolle die.
At si tale tibi studium natura paravit,
    Vivas ad antipodas – sis vel ut inde, redi!

Lycaon

Startled by your own snoring, Wolf, waking in a panic –
entangled in the underworld, you're exhausted by
nightly terrors at what gifts dawn might bring.
I can understand why you cringe at common daylight,
but if you're really just following the calling nature suited
you for, you'd be better off living in the Antipodes – or
rather, since you're from there, returning.

XXXIII

De sarcophago ubi turpia sculpta fuerant

Turpia tot tumulo defixit crimina Balbus,
    Post superos spurco Tartara more premens.
Pro facinus! Finita nihil modo vita retraxit!
    Luxuriam ad Manes moecha sepulcra gerunt.

33

Sarcophagus

The notorious Balbus, who furiously chiselled
all the filth he could on his own coffin –
as if he could pump and bugger the underworld
into some kind of submission. If he'd had time
to think, would he be ashamed of himself?
His recent death had no effect
on the continuing flow of that raucous life,
that coffin, like one of his erections
carried in solemn funeral procession
to a pale, insatiable tomb.

XXXIV

Item unde supra scriptum: ubi equi circi bibebant

Crevit ad ornatum stabuli circique decorem
    Puriot egregio reddita nymph loco
Quam cingunt variis insignia clara metallis
    Crispatumque super scinditur unda gradum.
Excipit hanc patuli moles miranda sepulcri,
    Corporibus vivis pocula blanda parans.
Nec iam sarcophagus tristis sua funera claudit,
    Sed laetos dulci flumine conplet equos.
Fundit aquas duro signatum marmore flumen,
    Falsa tamen species vera fluenta vomit.
Plaudite vos, Musae, diversaque, plaudite, signa,
    Quae circum docili continet arte decor,
Et dum palmiferis post praelia tanta quadrigis
    Garrula victores turba resolvit equos,
Praebete innocuos potus potusque salubres,
    Ut domino proprius gaudia circus agat.

34

Another Sarcophagus

A pure water spring has welled up, as if summoned
by the nymph of this place to bless and refresh
the horses of the racecourse. A graceful waterfall,

piped from a fountain surrounded by trophies
and caught in a magnificent huge coffin that
holds soothing drinks for breathing bodies.

Because this sarcophagus no longer sadly encloses the dead,
but swirls a sweet life giving stream to the horses.
An articifial channel of hard marble, that bubbles with

natural water. Muses, clap your hands. Applaud all you
gawking statues, bear witness to the beauty of skillful art.
And while the chattering crowd watches as the victorious

horses are unhitched for a healing drink from chariots
decorated with palms won in race after race; the owner
drinks to his own health and revels in the joy of the track.

In cinaedum bona sua corruptoribus dantem

Divitias grandesque epulas et munera multa,
    Quod proavi atque atavi quodque reliquit avus,
Des licet in cunctos et apargas, Becca, maritos,
    Plus tamen ille capit cui dare saepe cupis.
Nescio qui miserum et quod celas, Becca, Talento
    Vendere debueras, si bona membra dares.

The Heir

Important dinners, and parties, and bankrupting
feasts. All that substance your
grandfather, his father and your father
slowly harvested and gathered and turned
over to you. You try to toss out the good times
and the presents equally among your mates,
but lately there's a certain someone who's starting
to demand a little more from you. And you
find yourself wanting to give him what he wants.
I'm almost curious enough to ask you, Becca,
to take a look at what it is you've got hidden
under those robes. Because you normally
should be able... Becca, a *talent's* the market
price for a body in decent shape.

De eo qui uxorem prostare faciebat prop filiis habendis

Stirpe negata patrium nomen,
Non pater, audis; castus adulter
Coiugis castae viscera damnas,
Patriat spurcos ut tibi natos,
Inscia quo sint semine creti.
Fuerant forsan ista ferenda
Foeda, Proconi, vota parumper,
Scire vel ipsam si tuus umquam
Posset adultus dicere matrem.

36

You were denied the ability

of passing on your father's name.
But even though you're not
a father – they're calling you one.

As lovingly as any adulterer,
you condemned your wife's
chaste innermost parts to hell

so they could bear a spurious
son for you. And – because
you'd cleverly brought so many –

even she, herself, could never tell just
whose sperm it was he'd sprung from.
Maybe, for a little while yet,

this obscene marriage of yours
will be bearable. But, Proconius, will
your son when he's grown, be able

to say he remembers his mother,
or knows where she ended up?

De aletore in pretio lenocinii ludente

Ludis, nec superas, Ultor, ad aleam,
Nec quiquam in tabula das nisi virginem,
Spondens blanditias et coitus simul.
Hoc cur das aliis quod poteras tibi?
An tablae melius praelia grata sunt?
Aut prodest vitium tale quod impetras?
Si vincas, ego tre non puto virginem
In luxum cupere sed mage vendere.

Pimp Games

You play, Ultor, but hardly ever
win with those dice, and now
you've nothing of value left
to lay on the table except

a virgin who shyly promises
to come together, just petting. Why

give the others a chance at your prize?
Has gambling gotten sweeter than this nutty little
morsel? Or does your addiction abet your scheme?
If you were to win her back, Ultor, you'd need

to find some other way to market this virgin, who
you're not playing silly games with but selling.

XXXVIII

In nomen Aegyptii quo equi circi infortunium capiebant

Icarus et Phaeton, Veneto nolente, vocaris
    Atque Agilis, pigro cum pede cuncta premas.
Sed tamen et Phaethon cecidit super aethera flammis,
    Dum cupit insolitis nescius ire plagis.
Tu quoque confractis defectus in aequore pinnis,
    Icare, Phoebeo victus ab igne cadis.
Digna his ergo tibi praebentur nomina fatis,
    Per te iterum ut pereant qui periere prius.

38

Young Charioteer

"Icarus" and "Phaethon" they called you
when you went against the *Blues,*
and also just plain "Speed."

Then you tripped all over
your suddenly tangled feet.

When Phaetheon in his young
eagerness tried to travel in unknown places,
he dropped in flames from the high heavens.
You too, your wings broken, exhausted,

tumbled to the surface, "Icarus,"
under a blazing, godlike sun.
But you showed yourself worthy
of the honored names they gave you.
In you, the lost have gone to waste again.

XXXIX

De Romulo picto ubi in muris fratrem cecidit

Disce pium facinus – percusso, Romule, fratre,
Sic tibi Roma datur. Huius iam nomine culpet
Nemo te cedis, murorum si decet omen.

39

Divination

Recognize the difference, Romulus.
Yours was a pious crime.
When you struck
your brother down, Rome
gave herself to you.
Don't tolerate any criticism.
Don't let anyone
call it murder. Who's
going to bring charges
against a priest
prophesying on the walls.

XL

De eo qui amicos ad prandium clamabat ut plura expos-
ceret xenia

Gaudeo quod me nimis ac frequenter
Ambitu pascis Blumarit, superbo.
Unde sed pascor? Mea sunt per omnes
Sparsa convivas bona. Nec volebam
Pasceres quemquam peteresque mecum,
Ne tibi quiquam detur unde pascas,
Hoc tamen sed si vitio teneris,
Me precor numquam iubeas vocati.

40

Blumarit,

I'm glad you keep inviting me to your
tony dining circle. But what can I graze
on? My contribution is always
parcelled out among your guests; it
would be impolite to hoard. And I've
learned to be careful about eating what
you or anyone else brings on the excellent
chance it's spoiled. Please,
do me a favor, don't ask me again.

De auriga elato frequenter cadente

Pascasium aurigum populi forten esse fatentur
Ast ego no aliud quam turgida membra notabo
Inflatumque caput populis et amica ruinis
Brachia qua numquam recto moderamine frenant.
Mox cadit et surgit, rursam cadit, inde resurgit
Et cadit ut miseris frangantur crura caballis.
Non iste humano dicatur nomine natus;
Hunc potius gryphum proprium vocet Africo circo.

The public unanimously agrees: Pascasius

is a formidable driver. Yet I can't help noticing
the bruised body that goes along with his swollen head.
Because his powerful arms never seem able
to keep the bridle straight. But then, the public
always did love a crash. First he falls, then wrestles
them up. Falls again. Recovers. And falls
so pitifully he breaks his miserable horses' legs.
I don't think there's any human phrase to describe
him. I think we'd be better off just calling him
Africa's very own Griffin* of the Racing Circuit.

---

* The Griffin is a mythical creature with the head and wings of an eagle
and the body of a lion. It was a guardian of treasures and a fierce enemy
of horses.

De Laude aurigae Prasini

Iectofian, prasino felix auriga colore
    Priscorum conpar, ars quibus ipsa fuit,
Suetus equos regere et metas lustrare quadrigis
    Et quocumque velis ducere frena manu, –
Non sic Tantalides humero stat victor eburno.
    Una illi palma est, et tibi multa manet.

Iectofian

Lucky Iectofian, happy to be driving for the Greens,
as good as any of the master charioteers of legend
who ruled the racetrack as you rule your horses,
flying around the course just where you want them to go,
guided by your touch on the reins. Not even Tantalus'
gleaming son, Ivory-Shouldered Pelops outshines you.
He won – one prize. You have many yet to come.

XLIII

In eum qui foedas amabat

Diligit informes et foedas Myrro puellas.
    Quas aliter pulcro viderit ore, timet.
Iudicium hoc quale est oculorum, Myrro, fatere,
    Ut tibi non placeat Pontica, sed Garamas.
Iam tamen agnosco cur tales quaeris amicas.
    Pulcra tibi numquam, se dare foeda potest.

43

Myrro

really likes the ugly, dumpy girls
and actually seems afraid
of a pretty, pouting face.
Myrro, when a blonde from the Black Sea
doesn't please you,
but a Garamantian tribeswoman does,
you reveal something about either
your judgement or your eyesight.
Never mind, I've seen all along
what you look for in a lover.
A beauty would never, but an ugly
enough woman just might be capable
of subjecting herself to you.

XLIV

De simiis canum dorso inpositis

Reddita post longum Tyriis est mira voluptas,
    Quem pavet ut sedeat simia blanda canem.
Quanto magna parant felici tempora regno,
    Discant ut legem pacis habere ferae!

44

After too long, an astonishing show

has returned to perform for the Carthaginians.
Nervous, fawning monkeys somehow manage to stay
seated on the backs of fierce dogs. The fertile kingdom
may as well get ready for high times, even
wild animals are learning how the law keeps peace.

XLV

De partu ursae

Lambere nascentis fertur primordia prolis
    Ursa ferox, placido cum facit ore genus.
Expolit informes labris parientibus artus
    Et pietas subolem rursus amore creat.
Attrito truncum formatur corpore pignus,
    Ut sculpendo facit crescere membra faber.
Officium natura suum permisit amanti –
    Formam post uterum lingua magistra parit.

45

They say, that when the fierce bear gives birth, she gently

forms her baby with her mouth,
shines and polishes its pliant, shapeless body
with her lips and, with pious devotion,
once more, tenderly, creates another generation.

The way a master craftsman sculpts
a soft clay limb into life, she molds the flesh
of her exhausted, battered whelp
into something promising.

Nature has surrendered its good duty
to a loving creature – who licks things into shape
first with her uterus, and then
with her wise tongue.

XLVI

De laude horti Eugeti

Hortus quo faciles fluunt Napaeae,
Quo ludunt Dryades virente choro,
Quo fovet teneras Diana Nymphas,
Quo Venus roseos recondit artus,
Quo fessus teretes Cupido flammas
Suspensis reficit liber pharetris,
Quo sese Aonides ferunt puellas
Cui numquam minus est amoena frondis,
Cui semper redolent amoma verni,
Cui fons perspicuis tener fluentis
Muscoso riguum parit meatu,
Quo dulcis avium canor resultat –
Quidquid per varias refertur urbes,
Hoc uno famulans loco resultat.

46

The Garden:

Through which Napaeae quietly glide.
Where the green Dryad chorus plays, and
Diana still nurtures and protects her tender nymphs.
Where Venus sheathes her rosy body in the leaves.
Where weary Cupid hangs his quiver
and replenishes his gentle fire.
Where the muses are carried away by girlishness.
Whose lovely foliage never withers.
Whose lovely fragrance is a perpetual April
watered by a clear, gently rising spring
rippling through the moss.
Whatever the ever changing cities need brought
home to them, is all here in one place,
adaptable and at your service.

XLVII

De tablista furioso quasi tesseris imperante

Ludit cum multis Vatanans sed ludere nescit,
    Et putat imperio currere puncta suo.
Sed male dum numeros contraria tessera mittit,
    Clamat et irato pallidus ore fremit.
Tum verbis manisbusque furens miserandus anhelat,
    De solitis faciens proelia vera iocis.
Effundit tabulam, mensam, subsellia, pyrgum,
    Perditaque Haryacis aera rapit manibus.
Hic si forte unam tabulam non arte sed errans
    Vicerit aut aliam, nil bene dante manu,
Mox inflat venas et pallida guttura tendit
    Plisque furit vincens quam superatus erat.
Non iam huic, ludum sapientum calculus aptet,

    ....

47

The Luck of the Throw

Vantanas is always up for a game, but like any gambling
fool – thinks he can rule the dice. When they disobey and
betray him, he gets pale and mutters to choke back
his rage. Then with frantic words and gestures and pitifully
panting, he turns what's normally a trifle, into a real battle.
He explodes, overturns the board, the bench

the table, strews the dice cup, and with his Harpy hands
snatches at the empty air for his losses. This is the same guy,
who, when he manages to win – through no fault of his own, just
dumb luck – puffs himself up like an avenging conqueror.
He's no more suited for a game of skill...

....

XLVIII

De venatore picto in manibus oculos habente

Docta manus saevis quotiens se praebuit ursis,
    Numquam fallentem tela dedere necem.
Hinc etiam digitis oculos pictura locavit,
    Quod visum frontis provida dextra tulit.

48

The Eyes Painted on the Venator's Hands *

No matter how many times
he went hand to hand with the savage
bears, his spear never failed
to surprise them with death.
And so the painting even places
eyes on his fingers. Because,
his right hand saw more quickly
than the eye can see.

---

* A "venator" fought wild animals in the arena.

XLIX

Aliter unde supra

Venatori oculos manibus pictura locavit
    Et geminum egregia lumen ab arte manet.
Hic quocumque modo venabula fulgida pressit,
    Signatum veluti contulit exitium.
Naturae lucem vicerunt fortia facta.
    Iam visus proprios coepit habere manus.

49

The venator in the painting has eyes on his hands

and because the artist was extraordinary, the light
in the extra pair still radiates with life.
The way he twirled and feinted his flashing spear,
whatever he attacked was already marked for death.
His daring achievements outshone nature, now
his painted hands are beginning to develop
their own supernatural vision.

In aurigam effeminatum numquam vincentem

Praecidis, Vico, nec tamen praecedis,
Et quam debueras tenere partem,
Hac mollis misero teneris usu.
Umquam vincere possis ut quadrigis,
Corruptor tibi sit retro ponendus.

Premature Chariot

You always shoot out first and never last, Vico,
because you need to get hold of that part
you've softened with your pitiful, constant stroking.
The only time you're able to, somehow, hold
your horses, is when you let the sly guy,
who's paid you off, come from behind.

De paranympho delatore qui se ad hoc officium omnibus ingerebat

Hermes cunctormum thalamos et vota pererrat,
　　Omnibus ac sponsis pronunus esse cupit.
Hunc quisquam si forte velit contemnere dives,
　　Mox eius famam rodit iniqua ferens.
Nec tutum obsequiun nuptis. Famulatur amicis,
　　Indicet ut potius quae videt, ille nocens.
Non sua sortitur te qui facit auspice vota,
　　Sed tua, cui multum conferet ut taceas.

"Hermes,"

wanders between bedroom doors
and weddings and wants
to be the groom's best
man at every ceremony.
If anybody with money thinks
he can scorn him – ouch. It's
not long before Hermes
takes certain slanderous steps
to take a big bite from his
reputation. And don't think compliance
is going to save the groom. Hermes
is such an ingratiating friend, because
how else can he learn what he needs
to shake someone down. It's
not his own health, but yours –
Hermes – the groom is consulting
the auspices about. While he's solemnly
promising to pay whatever it costs
for your silence.

De funere mulieris formosae quae litigiosa fuit

Gorgoneos vultus habuit Catucia coniunx.
    Haec dum pulcra foret, iurgia saepe dabat.
Fecerat atque suum semper rixando maritum,
    Esset ut insano stultius ore tacens.
Et quotiens illam trepido cernebat amore,
    Horrebat, tamquam vera Medusa foret.
Defuncta est tandem haec iurgia ferre per umbras
    Cumque ipsa litem reddere Persephone.

The Wife,

Catucia had a face as fatally lovely
as a Gorgon's. But she was usually as angry
as she was gorgeous. She tore
right into her husband, who invariably
shut his crazy, fool mouth. When that poor
guy trembled and looked at his love,
he felt as trapped as if she were the true Medusa.
Now, she's finally done for – but he imagines her
still seething on the other side, demanding to be
sent back with Persephone in the spring.

LIII

De duobus qui se conpedibus quibus vincti erant ceciderunt

Conpedibus nexi quidam duo forte sedebant
    Criminis ob causam carceris ante fores.
Hi secum subitae moverunt iurgia rixae.
    Ebrietatis opus gessit iniqua fames.
Nec caedem pugnis aut calcibus egit uterque;
    Vincla illis telum, vincla fuere manus.
Nemo truces posthac debet pavitare catenas,
    Si reus e poenis* ingerit arma suis.

---

* poena – punishment – echoes Poeni – Carthaginian, native North
African ("Punic")

53

The Two Who Killed Each Other With Their Chains

They happened to be linked up
together, sitting in front
of the prison gate because of some
offense or other, when

suddenly their argument erupted, and
they began to brawl.
As if they were drunk, except it
was the work of that oppressive hunger.

They didn't break each other
to pieces with their fists or their
feet: they used their chains
to smash. Chains became their furious

grappling irons. So you see
after today, no one should feel obliged
to get into a panic over being arrested.
Not when prisoners can turn their
sentences into weapons they can hurl.

LIV

De causidico turpi qui concubam suam Charitem vocabat

Esset causidici si par facundia nervo,
    Impleret cuncti viscera negotii.
Ac tamen invigilat causis quae crimina pandunt-
    Cum Veneris famula iure Priapus agit.

54

If his lawyer's wits were as swift as his prick,

he'd get right to the bottom of every case. Notice
how he's constantly on the lookout for accusations
to look into and expose? When he goes to court to defend
Venus' girls – it's Priapus making the plea.

LV

In ministrum regis, qui alienas facultates vi extorquebat

Bella die nocteque suis facit Eutychus armis,
    Divitias cunctis e domibus rapiens.
Huic si forte aliquis nolit dare sive repugnet,
    Vim facit et clamat, "Regis habenda," nimis.
Quid gravius hostis, fur, aut latrunculus implet,
    Talia si dominus atque minister agit?

55

Eutychus

Eutychus makes armed war through
the night, confiscating the accumulated
wealth of all the houses. Yes, and if
someone won't hand it over, if anyone
tries to resist, he forces his way
and proclaims at the top of his voice,
"The King owns everything."
When a ruler and his officer
conduct themselves this way,
how much worse could invaders,
thieves, bandits be?

LVI

De eodem aliter

Cum famulis telisque furens penetralia cuncta
    Eutychus inrumpit divitasque rapit,
Hunc nullus vetat ire parens non forsan amicus;
    Deterior precibus redditus ille manet.
Quae sunt ergo manus aut ferrea tela ferenda,
    Quisve aries talem quodve repellat opus?
Huic si nemo potest ullas opponere vires,
    Obvia sint illi fulmina sola dei.

56

Eutychus

with his armed slaves bursts into the hearts of all the houses
and confiscates everything valuable. No patriarch or patron has
the authority to stop him: and pleading just makes him stay longer.
What hand, what iron weapon, what bulwark can be raised against
someone like this? No one has the power to mount
any opposition, and our only hope is the wrath of god.

*in eum, qui, cum senior dici nollet, multas sibi concubas
faciebat*

Accusas proprios cur longo ex tempore canos,
    Cum sis phoenicis grandior a senio,
Et quotiens tardam quaeris celare senectam,
    Paelicibus multis te facis esse virum?
Incassum reparare putas hac fraude iuventam –
    Harum luxus agit, sis gravior ut senior.

57

Why Prosecute

your own special shade of grey hair
created from lingering moments,
when you should be pleased
you've been allowed to become
such a venerable phoenix?

I mean how many times can you delay
the quick interrogations of old age
by proving you're still a man with
how many one-and-onlys on the side?

How did you ever conclude
you could recover the young days
with lies? The time you devote
to these out of control intrigues
just leaves you – if you please –
feeling ponderous as well as old.

LVIII

Item in supra scriptim quod se mori numquam diceret

Quantum tres Priami potuissent vivere mundo
    Aut quantum cornix atque elephans superest,
Tantam dum numeres longaeva aetate senectam,
    Te numquam firmas Tartara posse pati
Et credis Lachesim numquam tua rumpere fata
    Aeternoque putas stamine fila trahi.
Quamviz tarda, tibi veniet mors ultima tandem,
    Cum magis oblitus coeperis esse tui.
Nam poena est potius morbis producere vitam –
    Quod non semper habes, tristius, esse diu, est.

58

Now You Say You'll Never Die

As long as three Priams would have been able
to live on this earth, even longer than a crow or elephant –
that's how you calculate your longevity and senility.
You're sure, now, you'll never suffer the underworld,
have come to believe Lachesis will never snip your destiny,
think your threads will be woven and spun out forever.

Death will take its time with you, but will
finally take you; in the end a more thorough death.
Because you'll try, but will have already
forgotten who you are. Decay is the price
we pay for preferring to cling to life.
The longer we have what we
can't have forever, the sadder.

LIX

Epitaphion de filia Oageis infantula

Heu dolor! Est magnis semper mors invida fatis,
Quae teneros artus inimico sidere mergit!
Damira hoc tumulo regalis clauditur infans,
Cui vita innocua est quarto dirupta sub anno.
Nemo rosam albentem, fuerit nisi quae bona, carpit.

Haec parvam aetatem cuncta cum laude ferebat.
Grata nimis specie, verecundo garrula vultu
Naturae ingenio modicos superaverat annos.
Dulce loquebator, quidquid praesumpserat ore,
Linguaque diversum fundebat mellea murmur,
Tamquam avium verna resonat per tempora cantus.

Huius puram animam stellantis regia caeli
Possidet et iustis inter videt esse catervis.
At pater Oageis, Libyam dum protegit armis,
Audivit subito defunctam funere natam.
Nuntius hic gravior cunctis fuit hostibus illi,
Ipsaque sub tali flevit Victoria casu.

59

Epitaph for Oageis' Daughter

So much misery. Death always envies
magnificent destinies, baptizes their
tender limbs under a hateful star.
The royal child, Damira
is shut inside this grave, her innocent
life snapped before she was four.
How easily sadness blackens a pleasant lamp.
No one bothers picking
the white rose unless it's perfect.

She completed her short term with high
honors. Exceptionally pretty, bashful, chattering,
expressive: she was naturally ingenious
and well-behaved beyond her years.
Her voice was sweet, whatever the subjects
of her oratory, and her honeyed tongue
buzzed with a wealth of babbling as
resonant as song birds in a brief spring.

Obviously, her blameless soul has been claimed
by the heavenly kingdom in the stars, which keeps
an eye on her life among the righteous mob.
But her father, Oageis, got word of his daughter's
sudden death and burial while he was out, watching over
Libya with his army. The message he received there meant
more to him than all the hostiles who lived in the territory,
and Victory, herself, wept over such terrible luck.

LX

De amphitheatro in villa vicina mari fabricato

Amphitheatrales mirantur rura triumphos
    Et nemus ignotas cernit adesse feras.
Spectat arando novos agrestis turba labores
    Nautaque de pelago gaudia mixta videt.
Fecunus nil perdit ager, plus germina crescunt,
    Dum metuunt omnes hic sua fata ferae.

60

The new arena's promenade

astonishes the countryside
and the woods note the approach
of unfamiliar beasts. The struggling

farm laborers pause at their plowing
to examine the strange, passing mob,
and from the open sea, the boatmen eye

a jumble of delights. The abundant
fields lose nothing, the orchards
will bud all the better.

But the wild animals
watching from the trees
all shudder at their fate.

De sigillo Cupidinis aquas fundentis

Igne salutifero Veneris pur omnia flammans
  Pro facibus propriis arte ministrat aquas.

About those little statues

of Cupid squirting water.
You know – Venus' son –
the one who ignites all creation
with essential fire. See how
through the wonder of art
he wets it down.

De Neptuno in marmoreo alveo aquas fundente

Quam melio, Neptune, tuo sors ista tridente est.
　　Post pelagus dulces hic tibi dantur aquae!

62

Spouting Fountain

How much better off you are this way,
Neptune, than with your trident.
After the open seas,
they've given you fresh water.

De puteo cavata in monte arido

Quis hunc non credat ipsis dare Syrtibus amnes,
 Qui dedit ignotas viscere montis aquas?

63

The Mountain Well

Who wouldn't believe you could find rivers in the shifting sands
  after tapping a stream hiding in the heart of a bare mountain.

De aquis calidis Cirnensibus

Ardua montanos inter splendentia lucos
    Culmina et indigenis nunc metuenda feris,
Quo deserta prius solum nemus atra tenebat
    Tetraque inaccessam sederat umbra viam,
Qua vos laude canam quantoque in carmine tollam,
    In quibus extructa est atque locata salus?
Hic etiam ignitus tepet ad praetoria fervor,
    Plenior et calidas terra ministrat aquas.
....
....
Innocuos fotus membris parit intima tellus
    Naturamque pio temperat igne calor.
....
....

The Hotsprings at Cirne

High in the steep mountains among glowing groves
that were once home to fearsome animals who fear to go
there now; where once only a barely accessible road wound
through desolate dark forest: How can I sing your praise,
in what great ode, worthy of such a monument of health?
This is a palace where fire from the depths of the earth
gently warms the bubbling springs to the temperature of love

....

....

From its innocent most intimate parts the earth gives birth
to flame, then tempers its heat with piety...

....

....

LXV

De sententiis septem philosophorum distichi

Solon praecipuus, fertur qui natus Athenis,
Finem prolixae dixit te cernere vitae.

Chilon, quem patria egregium Lacadaemona misit,
Hoc prudenter ait te ipsum ut cognoscere possis.

Ex Mitylenaies fuerat qui Pittacus oris,
Te, ne quid nimis ut cupias, exquirere dixit.

Thales ingenio sapiens Milesius acri
Errorerm in terris firmat not caelitus esse.

Inde Prienaea Bias tellure creatus
Plures esse malos divina voce probavit.

Urbe Periander genitus, cui fama Corintho est,
Omnia constituit tecum ut meditando revolvas.

Cleobolus, proprium clamat quem Lindia civem,
Omne, inquit, magnum est quod mensura optima librat.

65

The Seven Sages

The legendary Solon, who, they say, was born in Athens pointed
out its only at the end, that you begin to understand a full life.

Chilon, the honored gentle patriot of Sparta, cautiously
advised: it's possible to get to know yourself.

But Pittacus, from the coast of Mitylene, said: neverthless,
you oughtn't to be too eager.

Thales of Milesius, that keen philosophic genius,
firmly asserted stupidity on earth isn't caused by heaven.

Then, from the countryside of Priene, Bias pronounced judgement
in a divine voice: most people are inherently evil.

Periander, born in famous Corinth, thought you could
solve anything by carefully thinking it over, and over.

According to Cleobulus, who Lindus claims as her very own,
the best measure of greatness is, always, equilibrium.

LXVI

De Ianuario mense

Lucifer annuorum et saeclie Sol, Iane, secundus.

 ....

Est rota certa tui tecum sine fine laboris;
 Itwue reditque tibi, quidquid in orbe venit.
Omnia perpetuis praecedis frontibus ora;
 Quae necdum venient quaeve fuere vides.

66

Janus

Morning star of each coming year –
century after century of suns –
Janus – how many countless thousand
nights have you passed through?
The course of your wheel
is fixed, but your work
is infinite: whatever comes to pass
in this world, leaves,
then returns with you.
Your eternally recurring kiss
greets every one
of your departing frowns.
You see all there ever
was – see what isn't
yet to be.

LXVII

De Olympio venatone Aegyptio

Grata voluptatis species et causa favoris,
Fortior innumeris, venator Olympie, palmis,
Tu verum nomen membrorum robore signas,
Alcides collo, scapulis, cervice, lacertis,
Admirande, audax, velox, animose, parate.
Nil tibi forma nocet nigro fuscata colore.
Sic ebenum pretiosum atrum natura creavit;
Purpura sic parvo depressa in murice fulget;
Sic nigrae violae per mollia gramine vernant;
Sic tetras quaedam conmendat gratia gemmas;
Sic placet obscuros elephans inmanis ad artus;
Sic turis piperisque Indi nigredo placessit;
Postremum tanto populi pulcrescis amore,
Foedior est quantum pulcher sine viribus alter.

67

Venator

The reason you're so popular is that we're grateful
for the show, Olympius, animal fighter. And
your name fits your gnarled body—with the neck,
shoulders, biceps and back of a Hercules.
Astonishing, quick, daring, impetuous and ready for anything,
that you're black doesn't hurt your looks a bit.
Nature created, dark, precious ebony. Royal purple
glimmers deep within the noble murex.
Blue-black violets blossom in the soft grass.
Dark jewels invest us with a special grace.
The dusky trunk of the terrible elephant thrills us.
Black incense and pepper from the Indies civilize
us. Need I say more? Scarred by your countless
wins, you're as beautiful in the people's love
as those elegant fops are hateful.

LXVIII

In epitaphion supra scripiti Olympii

Venator iucunde nimis atque arte ferarum
Saepe placens, agilis, gratus, fortissimus, audax,
Qui puer ad iuvenes dum no advixeris annos,
Omnia maturo conplebas facta labore.
Qui licet ex propria populis bene laude placeres,
Praestabas aliis ut tecum vincere possent.
Tantaque mirandae fuerant tibi praemia formae
Ut te post fatum timeant laudentque sodales.
Heu nunc tam subito mortis livore peremtum
Iste capit tumulus quem non Carthaginis arces
Amphitheatrali potuerunt ferre triumpho!
Sed nihil ad Manes hoc funere perdis acerbo.
Vivet fama tui post te longaeva decoris
Atque tuum nomen semper Carthago loquetur.

68

Epitaph for Olympius

No one was ever braver, venator, and your
absolute artistry with the savage beasts
thrilled us so very many times. But as much
as your audacity and agility, I remember how
gracious you were. Recall you as a boy, still too
young to shave, who cheerfully went to work
and matured in the unrelenting discipline of your trade.
And, even then – when the public began to recognize you,
to shower you with, well deserved, wild praise –
you always had that innate class, were always quick
to point out the share of others in your success.
You were blessed with such remarkable recuperative gifts
that, horrendous as your death was, your burial club hesitated
to order the funeral orations. Well, it's all too true.
You won't revive. Livid death has suddenly carried you off,
has trapped you in this little mound – you who all Carthage
couldn't catch when they tried to carry you in triumph
around the Arena. But really, Olympius, it's nothing
but the bitterness we burn to ashes on the funeral pyre.
Your glory will live to an honored old age, and Carthage
will always murmur your name.

LXIX

De Chimæra aenea

Aeris fulgiduli nitens metallo
Ignes pertulit, ante quos vomebat,
Et facta est melior Chimæra flammis.

69

The Bronze Chimæra

The ore has become glowing, brilliant
bronze by passing through the flames
she spewed from her mouth. The Chimæra,
perfected, forged in her own fire.

De statua Veneris in cuius capite violae sunt natae

Cypris candidulo reddita marmore
Veram se exanimis corpore praebuit.
Infudit propriaa membra caloribus,
Per florem in statuam viveret ut suam.
Nec mendax locus est. Qui violas forent
Servabit famulas inguinibus rosas.

The Flowering Venus

A smooth marble Cyprian returns to blush
and reveal her truth through a breathless
body. She pours her own special heat
into every part of the statue until
it comes alive with flowers.
No need to lie about where.
A violet doorway whose delicay is
guarded by a swell of handmaiden roses.

In caecum qui pulcras mulieres tactu noscebat

Lucius egenus, viduae frontis,
Iter amittens, caecus amator
Corpora tactu mollia palpat
Et muliebres iudicat artus
Nivei cui sit forma decoris
Credo quod ille nolit habere
Oculos per quos cernere possit,
Cui dedit plures docta libido.

The Blind Man at the Brothel

In need of some light, losing
his way, the blind, uncertain
lover with the widowed face gently
touches and strokes the skin
and examines the limbs
of the women, to judge, for himself,

which are the most
beautiful, which are snow white.
Skillful lust has given him
so many eyes, why should he want
two more, simply to see?

In philosophum hirsutum nocte tantum cum puellis concumbentem

Hispidus tota facie atque membris,
Crine non tonso capitis verendi,
Omnibus clares Stoicus magister.
Te viris tantum simulas modestum
Nec die quaeris coitum patrare
Ne capi possis lateasque semper.
Fervidus sed cum petulante lumbo
Nocte formosas subigis puellas.
Incubus fies subito per actus,
Qui Cato dudum fueras per artes.

The Tutor

With fur sprouting everywhere
on your face and from your collar,
and with your carefully unbarbered,

venerably shaggy head, everyone
recognizes the shining personification
of a distinguished Stoic schoolmaster.

You're careful to maintain that image
of a modest, unassuming man and there's
not even a question of getting together

to do the deed during the day.
You dread being caught too much.
Even though you've always been good

at never being noticed. But in the
feverish middle of the night, you teach
the so beautiful young girls their real

lessons with your insolent grinding
hips, as you're suddenly thrust into the role
of an insatiable incubus.

When only a little earlier
you were earnestly philosophizing
about the principles of Cato.

LXXIII

De catula sua brevissima ad domini sui nutum currente

Forma meae catulae brevis est sed amabilis inde,
    Hanc totam ut possit concava ferre manus,
Ad domini vocem famulans et garrula currit,
    Humanis tamquam motibus exiliens.
Nec monstrosum aliquid membris gerit illa decoris;
    Ombnibus exiguo corpore visa placet.
Mollior huic cibus est somnusque in stramine molli.
    Muribus infensa est, saevior atque catis.
Vincit membra nimis latratu parvola torvo.
    Si natura daret, posset ab arte loqui.

73

My puppy is so delightful because

she's so small. I'm actually able to hold
all of her in the hollow of my hands.
She's a faithful servant, who runs
to her master's voice and sits up
with almost human movements.
And not one of those overbred,
miniature monstrosities: everyone agrees
her naturally lean, little body
is a simple pleasure to behold.
Her meals are refined, and she dozes
on the finest straw. To mice, she's
a relentless enemy, and a savage
to crafty cats. She compensates
for being a pup by barking,
excessively and fiercely,
but would rather, if nature permitted,
break out in eloquent speech.

LXXIV

De pardis mansuetis qui cum canibus venantionem faciebant

Cessit Lyaie sacra fama numinis
Lynces ad oris qui subegit Indicis.
Curru paventes duxit ille bestias
Mero gravatas ac minari nescias
Et quas domarent vincla coetu garrulo.
Sed mira nostri forma constat saeculi;
Pardos feroces saeviores tigribus
Praedam sagaci nare mites quaerere
Canum inter agmen et famem doctos pati,
Quidquid capessunt ore ferre baiulo,
O qui magister terror est mortalium,
Diros ferarum qui retundit impetus,
Morsum repertis ut cibis non audeant!

74

Bacchus, who harnessed wild lynxes in India, has ceded

his divine reputation: The panicked animals who
drew the god's chariot were plied with unwatered wine
until they were no threat to anyone. And even then,
they were a noisy bunch.

But we've perfected an amazing art form in our age.
Leopards as fierce as savage tigers, quietly run
with the keen scented hounds as they hunt their prey.
They're trained to ignore their hunger and carry
back whatever they catch like porters.

What a master the terror of mortal men
can be. It blunts the attack of the most
dreadful beasts, so that they lose
the courage to take even a bite
of the meal in their mouth.

LXXV

In psaltiam foedam

Cum saltas misero, Gattula, corpore
Hoc cuiquam libitum est, horrida, quod facis,
Insanam potius te probo psaltriam
Quae foedam faciem motibus ingraves
Et, dum displiceas, quosque feras iocos.
Credis quod populos cymbala mulceant?
Nemo idicium tale animi gerit
Pro te ut no etiam gaudia deserat.

75

Gattula:

when you jump up and dance, how does
your pathetic body give pleasure to anyone, ruffian?
What you're doing just proves you'd better stick to being
a crazy musician: – hunched over the psalter, your scowling
face dark with emotions. Never satisfied with yourself,
everyone's cruel joke, you think. Do you think people
are charmed by the cymbals, that no one has enough
sophistication to forgo even such pleasures for you?

LXXVI

Item de ea quod ut amaretur praemia promittebat

Quid facis ut pretium promittens, Gattula, ameris?
  Da pretium ne te oderis ipsa simul!
Praemia cur perdis? Cur spondes munera tantis?
  Accipe tu pretium ne mihi dona feras!
Non est tam petulans pariterque insanus amatofr
  Qui te non credat prodigiale malum.
Sed si forte aliquis moechus surrexit ab umbris,
  Cui talis placeas, huic tua dona dato!

76

Why are you offering to pay

for love, Gattula? Isn't it worth more
not to hate yourself? And why
promise to pay that much, just
for another disaster? Do me a favor:
don't pay me. Because you won't
find a lover either crazy or presumptuous
enough to not be convinced
you're up to some prodigious mischief.
But if a certain sleazy character
who delights you so much,
happens to rise from the dead –
you'll have to pay the price again.

In ebriosam et satis meientem

Quod bibis et totum dimittis ab inguine Bacchum,
    Pars tibi superior debuit esse femur.
Potabis recto – poteris, Follonia, – Baccho,
    Si parte horridius infereiore bibas.

When you booze like this

and need to pee, you always say you're going
to let some of the wildness out. It flows
between your legs, Follonia – so your cleared mind
owes a certain debt to your thighs.
Pay it back, Follonia – you know how. Let's
quench your wild bottom's boozy thirst.

In mulierem pulcram castitati studentem

Pulcrior et nivei cum sit tibi forma coloris,
  Cuncta pudicitiae iura tenere cupis.
Mirandum est quali naturam laude gubernes
  Moribus ut Pallas, corpore Cypris eas.
Te neque coniugii libet excepisse levamen;
  Saepius exoptas nolle videre mares.
Haec tamen est animo quamvis exosa voluptas:
  Numquid non mulier conparis esse potes?

78

Especially, with that precious,

snow-white skin, you know
how desirable your body is, but all
you seem to desire is to conform
to all the icy rules of chastity.
It's wonderful, the way
you, so commendably, govern
your contradictory nature,
that you can live like Pallas Athena,
with the body of the Cytherean. No,
you don't think it would be nice
to catch some nice man to live with;
you long for the day you could, completely,
avoid men's looks. And yet, voluptuous
longings (no matter how you detest them)
keep quickening in your soul. Isn't there any
other woman like yourself?

De eo qui, cum Burdo diceretur, filiae suae Pasiphaae nomen inposuit *

Disciplinarum esse hominem risusque capacem,
    Quod nulli est pecudi, dixit Aristoteles.
Sed cum Burdo homo sit, versum est sophistmate verum.
    Nam et ridere solet vel ratione viget.
Surrexit duplex nostro sub tempore monstrum:
    Quod pater est burdo Pasipaeque redit.

---

* The title writer suggests a daughter named Pasiphae as an explanation for the poem. An alternate reading might ascribe the Pasiphae image (rather than name) to the mother. Her bestiality, albeit, with an ass rather than bull.

Burdo and his New Child

Humanity is capable of learning and laughter,
capacities no other animal shares: So said Aristotle.
But with "Burro" the man, philosophy becomes sophistry.
He can snigger and he's smart as a whip. Yet, here
we have – a double aberration. The father
is a sterile mule. And Pasaphaeque's come back to earth.

De laude rosae centumfoliae

Hanc puto de proprio tinxit Sol aureus ortu
    Aut unum ex radiis maluit esse suis.
Sed si etiam centum foliis rosa Cypridis extat,
    Fluxit in hanc omni sanguine tota Venus.
Haec florum sidus, haec Lucifer almus in agris.
    Huic odor et color est dignus honore poli.

80

Centofilia

I imagine it's been imbued with the tint
of dawn by the golden sun as it rises, wishing
it could claim it as one of its rays.
But it's also known as the Cypriot's
hundred petal rose and it's permeated
with all of Venus' pulsing blood.
This is the proud flower, the gracious
morningstar of the meadow. Its fragrance,
its blush, merit heaven's respect.

De statua Hectoris in Ilio, quae videt Achillem et sudat

Ilion in medium Pario de marmore facti,
Stant contra Phrygius Hector vel Graius Achilles.
Priamidae statuam sed verus sudor inundat
Et falsum fictus Hector formidat Achillem.
Nescio quid mirum gesserunt Tartara saeclo.
Credo quod aut superi animas post funera reddunt
Aut ars mira potest legem mutare barathri.
Sed si horum nihil est, certe extat marmore Hector
Testaturque suam viva formidine mortem.

Two Statues

They've put up two statues in the town
square of Troy. Sculpted from Parian
marble, Trojan Hector and Greek Achilles
stare at each other. And
once again, a symbolic Hector is threatened
by a make-believe Achilles.
Except Priam's son is drenched
with actual sweat.

The gray kingdom of the dead has finally
accomplished its first miracle.
Or is it those other mysterious
spirits – who, they say, stand above and
behind human life – who've taken to forcing corpses
back into existence from the grave?

Why bother with
explanations that don't make sense:
the image of Hector remains, remembering
the ritual of his death with living fear.

De muliere Marina vocabulo

Quidam concubitu futuit fervente Marinam;
    Fluctibus in salsis fecit adulterium.
Non hic culpandus, potius se laude ferendus,
    Qui memor est Veneria quod marfe nata foret.

82

Marina

A certain person lay down to dinner with
and ended up fucking boiling Marina.
Now the adultery is making some salty waves.
Not only should this affair not be
condemned. If possible, it should,
in fact, be commemorated.
Because it reminds us that Venus,
the daughter of the sea, somehow, still lives.

De horto domni Oageis, ubi omnes herbae medicinales plantate sunt

Constructas inter moles parietibus altis
    Hortus amoenus inest aptior et domino.
Hic vario frondes vitales semine crescunt
    In quibus est Genio praemedicante salus.
Nil Phoebi Asclepique tenet doctrina parandum:
    Omnibus hinc morbis cura sequenda placet.
Iam puto quod caeli locus est ubi numina regnant,
    Cum datur his herbis vincere mortis onus.

In a Hidden Courtyard

behind massive walls
is a garden whose contents
are useful to its master.
Here, seeds containing
a living Djinn sprout into plants
and ripen into remedies that
keep you in good health.
There's no need to consult
the *Phoebian* textbooks
or send for anything else.
Everything you need to cure
an illness in an orderly manner
is right here.
I've come to believe
it's a celestial place
ruled by a divine presence.
With the help of these herbs
it's possible to overcome
the burden of death.

De pica quae humanas voces imitabatur

Pica hominum voces cuncta ante animalia monstrat
    Et docto externum perstrepit ore melos.
Nec nunc oblita est quidnam prius esset in orbe;
    Aut haec Picus erat aut homo rursus inest.

Pica

This pet little magpie,
trained to chatter away
in a tongue that's foreign to its beak,
is first among the animals
at mimicking human speech.

Because it still remembers what it was
in this world, before turning
into itself. Because this is either Prince
Picus * who scorned the goddess –
or some other poor human, incarnate.

---

* In Ovid's *Metamorphoses* Picus was propositioned by Circe in the
forest. When he rejected her because he wanted to be faithful to
his young wife, Circe promptly changed him into a woodpecker (a
"picus"), so that all that would be left of him was his name. The
"pica" – a species of magpie, not a true woodpecker, was commonly
trained to speak like a parakeet in antiquity.

De rustica in disco facta, quae spinam tollit de plant satyri

Cauta nimis spinam satyri pede rustica tollit,
    Luminibus certis vulneris alta notans.
Illum panduri solatur voce Cupido,
    Inridens tali vulnere flere virum.
Nil falsum creas artem lusisse figuris;
    Vivi minus speciem reddere membra solent.

Figures on a Plate

How cautiously the country girl lifts the thorn
out of the Satyr's foot. All the while clucking,
scolding the unquestionably horrible gash.
Cupid, dressed up like a flute player
stands there muttering his ridiculous consolations:
A grown man crying? Moaning
over a little cut like that? And where
does art borrow to lend this kind
of life to the stock figures? Real
human beings are hardly this vital.

De colocasia herba in tecto populante

Nilus quam riguis parit fluentis
Extendens colocasia ampliores
Ramos, per spatium virens amoenum,
Haec nostris laribus creata frondet.
Naturam famulans opaca vertit
Plus recto ut vigeat solet quam horto.

86

It comes from the gently flowing

waters of the Nile, this spreading lotus,
eager to fill the room with pleasure,
to grow its green leaves and flower
in this blessed home of ours.
Adapting itself to the shadows,
it confounds nature and thrives
better, hidden here, than
it ever could in a garden.

De eo qui podium amphitheatri saliebat

Amphitheatralem podium transcendere saltu
Velocem audivi iuvenem nec credere quivi
Hunc hominem, potius sed avem, si talia gessit.
Et posui huic, fateor, me Dorica vina daturum
Conspicere ut possem tanti nova facta laboris.
Aspexi victusque dedi promissa petenti
Atque meo gravior levis extitit ille periclo.
Non iam mirabor sumtis te, Dedale, pinnis
Isse per aetherios natura errante meatus.
Hunc magis obstipui coram qui plebe videnti
Corpore, non pinnis, fastigia summa volavit.

The Arena Acrobat

At the Amphitheater I overheard a quick young
man declare he could leap above the podium.
Impossible, I thought, unless he flew like
a bird. So, I staked him, I confess, to a flagon
of Doric wine. And realized I'd been had as he
pulled himself over the balcony rail, then scampered off,
light enough despite the weight of his prize.
Daedalus, I won't marvel so much at your errant
wanderings through the skies, defying nature.
I'm more astonished now at the way these characters
fly without wings from the cheap seats to the best.

De Diogene picto, ubi lascivienti menetrix barbam evillit et Cupido mingit in podice eius

Diogenem meretrix derisum Laida monstrat
    Barbatamque comam frangit amica Venus.
Nec virtus animi nec castae semita vitae
    Philosophum revocat turpiter esse virum.
Hoc agit infelix, alios quo saepe notavit.
    Quodque nimis miserum est: mingitur arte sophus.

In the painting, Diogenes

is being made a silly fool of by Lais,
the prostitute. His fuck friend is
putting a queer wave in the bearded one's moustache.

Neither his manly soul, nor his abstinent life
in the streets deter the great philosopher from
being a ridiculous man. And look – closer –

isn't this just how that unhappy character
often scorned others? Art – in this
pathetic little scene – pisses on the wise.

De catto, qui, cum soricem maiorem devorasset, apoplexiam passus occubuit

Immensi soricis cattus dum membra vorasset
    Deliciis periit crudior ille suis.
Pertulit adsuetae damnum per viscer praedae;
    Per vitam moriens concipit ore necem.

89

Cattus

When the cat dismembered and gulped
the great shrew mouse down, it perished,
poisoned by this indigestible delicacy.
It died, putting the nourishment
it needed to live in its mouth,
condemned to its final agony by the instincts
of its predatory heart.

In Anclas; in salutatorium domini regis

Hildirici regis fulget mirabile factum
    Arte, opere, ingenio, divitiis, pretio,
Hinc radios sol ipse capit quos huc dare possit.
    Altera marmoribus creditur esse dies.
Hic sine nube solum; nix iuncta et sparsa putatur.
    Dum steterint, credas mergere posse pedes.

90

Hilderic's Palace *

This marvelous achievement
of King Hilderic is so bright,
inspired and cleverly built,
so intricately decorated and expensive,
that the sun refreshes itself
here as if in a mirror and you'd think
a second day was breaking out of the polished
marble, think you're in those cloudless
mountains where glittering snow
lies thick and icy everywhere.
And even standing still, you can't help but imagine
your feet are sliding out from under you.

---

* Hilderic was the penultimate Vandal king, deposed and killed by his
cousin, Gelimer, who was then himself overthrown by the Byzantine
invasion that ended the Vandal Empire.

Sol, qui terrarum flammis opera omnia lustrat,
Exulit os sacrum caelo tenbrasque resolvit.
 Laetitia ludisque viae plausuque fremebant,
At Venus aetherios inter dea candida nimbos
Aurea subnectens exertae cingula mammae,
Dona ferens, pacem aeternam pactosque hymenaeos
Atque omnem ornatum, capitolia celsa tenebat,
Punica regna videns, Tyrios et Agenoris urbem.
Hinc atque hinc glomerantur Oreades et bona Iuno.
Incedunt pariter pariterque ad limina tendunt.
Tectum angustum, ingens, centum sublime columnis,
Hae sacris sedes epulis, atque ordine longo
Perpetuis soliti patres considere mensis.
Una omnes, magna iuvenum stipante caterva,
Deveniunt faciemque deae vestemque reponunt.
Dant signum, fulsere ignes et conscius aether
Conubiis, mediisque parant convivial tectis.
Fit strepitus tectis vocemque per ampla voluntat
Atria abi adsuetis biforem dat tibia cantum..
At tuba terribilem sonitum procul aere canoro
Increpuit mollitque animos et temperat iras.
It clamo caelo, cithara crinitus Iopas
Obloquitur numeris septem discrimina vocum,
Iamque eadem digitis, iam pectine pulsat eburno.
Nec non et Tyrii per limnina laeta frequentes
Convere, toris iussi discumbere pictis.
Tunc Venus aligerum dictis affatur Amorem:
"Nate meae vires, mea magna potential solus,
"Huc geminas nunc flecte acies, illam aspice contra.
"Quae vocat insignus facie viridique iuventa,
"Iam matura viro, iam plenis nubilis annis,
"Cui genus a proavis ingens clarumque patenae
"Nomen inest virtutis et nota maior imago.

91

[Cento]

The Sun, who lights up at once the world below,
Raises his sacred head in heaven banishing darkness.
The fields resound with shouts, the streets with praise,
And Venus, bright goddess among heaven's clouds,
Throws across her naked breast a golden belt,
To come bearing wedding gifts and everlasting peace,
And stands upon the lofty capitol, surveying Punic lands,
the Carthaginians and the city of Agenor.
All around gather the Orieades, as kindly Juno
Leads them likewise through the dancing threshold
Into the stately hall where a hundred pillars shine,
And at long tables the sacred feast is set,
While in their ranks the godlike grandsires stood.
A clamoring throng of youths crowds all around,
As the goddesses undo their aspects and shining garments.
The signal given, lightning flashes across the aether,
And the feast is prepared within the palace,
Sounds of revelry and voices fill the large halls
And to the music of their pipes the Phrygians go
And now the trumpets blast terrible from afar,
With rattling clangor, rouse the sleepy war.
Shouts rend the skies, long-haired Iopas accompanying,
His flying fingers and harmonious quill
Strike seven notes and seven intervals they fill.
In great number the Carthaginians crowd the halls,
Invited to gather and sit on the painted couches.
Then Venus speaks to winged Cupid:

"My son, my strength, primal source of my powers
Turn your eyes this way and look at her.
Fired with love, and blooming with beauteous youth,

"Hoc opus, hic labor est; thalamus ne desere pactos!
"Credo equidem, nova mi facies inopinave surgit. "Nonne vides,
quantum egregio decus enitet ore?
"Os humerosque deo similis, cui láctea colla
"Auro innectuntur, crines nodantur in aurum,
"Aurea purpuream subnectit fibula vestem.
"Qualis gemma micat, quails Nereia Doto
"Et Galatea secant spumantem pectore pontum.
"Cura mihi comitumque foret nun una mearum!
"Hanc ego nunc ignaram huius quodcumque pericli est,
"Cum tacet omnis ager, noctem non amplius unam
"Conubio iungam stabili propriamque dicabo.
"Hic Hymenaeus erit monumentum et pignus amoris.
"Incipe se qua animo virtus, et consere detxram
"Occultum inspires ignem paribusque regamus
"Auspiciis: liceat Frido serviré marito,
"Cui natam egregio genero dignisque hymenaeis
"Dat pater et pacem hanc aeterno foedere iungit."
Paret Amor dictis carae genetricis et alas
Exuit et gressu gaudens sic ore locutus:
"Mecum erit iste labor; si quid mea numina possunt,
"Cum dabit amplexus atque oscula dulcia figet
"Inmiscentque manus manibris pugnamque lacessunt,
"Nusquam abero, solitam flamman (datur hora quieti)
"Desuper infundam et, tua si mihi certa voluntas,
"Omnia praccepi atque animo mecum ante peregi
 "Sentiet!" atque animu praesenti firmat.
Illa autem (neque enim fugu iam super ulla pericli est)
Cogitur et supplex animos summittere amori.
Spemque dedit dubaie menti solvitque pudorem.
Illum turbat amor; ramum qui veste latebat
Eripit a femine et flagranti fervidus infert.
It cruor inque humeros cervix conlapse recumbit.
His demum exactis geminam dabit Illia prolem,
Laeta deum partu, centum conplexa nepotes.

Ripe for marriage and now of proper age,
Her lineage mighty, her father a chief of ancient blood.
This thy task and mighty labor; do not desert the promised bed!
Certainly I believe a wondrous shape took place before me.
Behold you not what uncommon grace that mouth bestows?
Countenance and shoulders like a god, milk-white neck
Ringed in gold, her flowing hair a golden caul restrains,
A golden clasp her Tyrian robe sustains. She shines a gem,
like Dotis and Galatea and the daughters of the sea
Cleaving with their breasts the watery deep.
That she were dear to me, and one of my celestial train.
In but a single night, when the countryside is still,
I shall unite her, unaware of whatever peril,
In steadfast marriage and declare her to be his.
This wedding shall be a shrine and pledge of love.
Begin if there be courage in your heart, and draw close.
Breathe secret fire in her and let us rule with equal auspices:
Grant her serve her husband, Fridus, uncommon son-in-law,
to whom in fitting marriage her father gives her,
with a lasting peace and binding wedding rites."

Cupid heeds his dear mother's words and lays aside
His wings and joyously walks forth saying:
"Mine be that task; if my divine will is still able
As he embraces her and gives her sweet kisses
And they engage hand to hand and provoke battle.
I shall never leave them, and from above I shall pour
The wonted flame of passion (the hour given to rest)
And, if thy will be mine, I have so foreseen
Everything and sought it out with all my mind.
She shall know."

And with this pledge cheers her spirit.
Yet the bride (for no longer is she to escape her peril)
Considers submitting her spirit humbly to love.

Giving hope to a wavering mind she rids herself of scruples.
Afire with love he shows the rod concealed within his cloak
And raging with desire gives to his glowing bride.
Blood flows, her snowy neck reclines upon her breast.
This done, Ilia will give birth to twins and rejoice
In the divine and noble progeny that she has bred.

(trans. by Rocío Carlos & Paul Vangelisti)

Epitaphion

Nil mihi mors faciet: pro me monumenta relinquo,
Tu modo vive, liber: nil mihi mors faciet.

Epitaph *

To me, death's nothing: in place
of myself, I'll leave a monument. Live
if you can, book: to me, death's nothing.

---

* *Anthologia Latina,* anonymous but sometimes attributed to Luxorius

Decompressing Luxorius: Translation Issues

PREVIOUS TRANSLATORS

Anyone wanting to translate Luxorius would do well to begin with Morris Roseblum's 1961 Columbia University Press study, *Luxorius, A Latin Poet Among the Vamdals*. Rosenblum's book is a comprehensive piece of scholarship. Along with historical background and discussions of various Luxorius interpretations, Roseblum includes something invaluable to non-linguist translators: a complete index of the nouns and verbs in the poems, including Latin cases and roots. He also identifies questionable words, with choices for possible emendation.

Rosenblum's translations, however, are prose trots that often seem to miss the points and ironies of the poem. His approach is so conservative that, in some cases, he refuses to try to make sense of a poem, leaving his readers as well as himself, scratching their heads.

Except for scattered pieces, the only significant number of literary translations I'm aware of are those by Jack Lindsay who included thirteen Luxorius poems in his 1948 Late Latin anthology, *Song of a Falling World*. Lindsay's approach, casting the poems in end line rhyme, is different than mine and I'd encourage any interested reader to explore how interpretations can differ.

FORM AND VOICE

Classical Latin poetry was formal, but metric, not rhymed, and based on patterns of "long" and "short" syllables not generally amenable to modern European languages. While rhyme can be found in, say, Horace, it's as incidental embellishment, not as form. Despite this, there's a long tradition in English of translating Latin poems into various end line rhyme schemes. I think this was the case for a couple of reasons.

One is that well into the 19th century, Latin was a basic part of the English school curricula. John Dryden's 17th century audience had, for the most part, been taught to read Horace in the original. They didn't need a direct translation. What Dryden and others did was to "English" Horace, to attempt to create a poem that sounded as if it were a poem written in their own language.

But if the Latin poem were to pass muster as an English poem, it had to make use of the poetics of the day. This is what makes the imposition of a form in translation that's foreign to the original so tricky. It's valid to argue that, for example, Rilke's sonnets are best translated into English in some variation of the sonnet form. Or that Dryden, translated into French, should arrive in couplets.

Conversely, though, when Dryden imposes his couplets on Horace the result, while lovely, exiles Horace to the 17th century where he's in danger of losing his voice in Dryden's anachronistic voice.

Some level of anachronism is unavoidable when trying to translate across fifteen hundred years. But I wanted to avoid this as much as possible with Luxorius, aware that I was trying to capture a moment in history as well as a poem – and that with Luxorius, the two seemed indivisible. So my preference was for a verse as prosaic and unobtrusive as possible, on the theory that plain speech is the best time and culture traveler. That said, Luxorius' energy derives from the specifics of sixth-century Roman Africa. The race has to be run with Luxorius' horses and his own arena where he remains a tricky fellow to catch.

In addition to the cultural chasms between "then" and "now," Luxorius often writes in a Latin so compressed as to be almost code. Latin, even at its most expansive, is much more compact than English. (Compare the single-volume Oxford Latin Dictionary to the shelf-long OED.) With most Latin writers the problem is choosing the one right word from the dozen or more English words one Latin word might mean. With Luxorius, it often goes beyond that almost to the point of unfolding a stone. Take the following three line poem, #39.

> *De Romulo picto ubi in muris fratrem cecedit.*
>
> *Disce pium facinus – percuccom Romule fratre,*
> *Sic tibi Roma datur. Huius iam nomine culpet*
> *Nemos te c(a)edis, murorum si decet omen.*

The appended title imagines that the poem is describing a painting of Romulus killing his brother Remus on the walls of Rome. To restate the old legend, the wolf-suckled twins Romulus and Remus founded Rome, and Romulus then walled the nascent City. Remus, mocking his brother, leapt over the walls. Whereupon, Romulus killed him and became the sole ruler of Rome.

The poem makes no mention of a painting and it's hard to imagine what such a representation would be like. A word for word rendering might read as follows:

> *Understand the crime was pious: Struck Romulus, your brother,*
> *By this means Rome was given to you. How can anyone call reproach,*
> *no one, you make a sacrificial murder, walls if proper omen.*

Rosenblum grammatically expands:

Realize that yours was a virtuous crime, Romulus. When you struck down your brother, Rome was given to you by that act. Let no one now accuse you of this deed as murder, if the omen of the walls proves what you did was right.

Rosenblum also points out that Luxorius' last line is a palindrome, i.e., it reads identically backward and forward. (The slight imperfection is the omitted implicit "a" in *caedo*, to kill, murder, and also sacrifice.) This is, I believe, the only instance in Luxorius of this rather artificial, Late Latin grammarian's conceit.

In our era, we're used to looking for poetic effect in the sound and rhythm of words. Luxorius, with this palindrome, pursues a somewhat different poetics, a layering of images. In essence, he seems to be creating a mirror image within a mirror, an echo, not with sound, but with an almost mathematical arrangement of letters, as if he were casting a spell or invoking the spirits. The key to this poem, I think, is in the first word, *discerno* – to "discern" but to do so by "separating," "distinguishing," the way an ancient Roman priest of Romulus' time might study entrails. Because the palindromic last line with its "omen" and "sacrifice" incorporates a prophecy in which the future is mirrored in the past and the past in the future, so that the line circles itself and can be read backwards as well as forwards.

One could (and Luxorius did) write this poem in three Latin lines. I don't know how it could be done in English. The palindrome is more than a line, more than two lines; it's a doubling back on itself of *the entire poem.* The approach I took – and it's certainly not the only one possible – was to expand and "explain" the poem a little with "describing" it. No less than the 8th century copyist, I thought a title might help.

Divination

Recognize the difference, Romulus.
Yours was a pious crime.
When you struck

your brother down, Rome
gave herself to you.
Don't tolerate any criticism.
Don't let anyone
call it murder. Who's
going to bring charges
against a priest
prophesying on the walls?

This isn't Luxorius' three-line poem. It's his song, if you will, transcribed for a totally different instrument. For better or worse, I've come to think poetic "voice" is as much, if not more, a matter of perspective as tone or sound. Hopefully, I haven't tampered much with the uniqueness, or "foreignness," of that perspective.

TRANSLATING THE UNSPEAKABLE

Probably a quarter of Luxorius' poems deal with sex, sometimes at least on surface, with sexual vituperation. That surface reading by classicists who often seem disinterested in or dismissive of Late Latin poets may have something to do with Luxorius reputation as a "decadent." Luxorius' #31 is, on surface, outrageously obscene. Moreover, both Roseblum and the noted classicist D.R. Shackleton-Bailey seemed to find the epigram's point to be somewhat obscure.

In Puellam Hermaphroditam

Monstrum feminei bimembre sexus,
Quam coacta virum facit libido,
Quin gaudes futui furente cunno?
Cur te decipit impotens voluptas?
Non das, quo pateris facisque, cunnum,
Ilam, qua mulier probaris esse,
Partem cum dederis, puella tunc sis.

Rosenblum's bowdlerized translation actually seems cruder than Luxorius' unblushing Latin, paradoxically, I think, because Rosenblum is ready to take literally what he sees as a prime example of late antiquity decadence.

> *To a Hermaphrodite Girl: Two-organed monster of the female sex, whom enforced lust turns into a man, why do you not enjoy the normal way of making love? Why does violent, vain pleasure deceive you? You do not give that which you are passive and also active. When you offer that part of you which proves you are a female, then you may be a girl.*

For me, the clue to this poem is in the two straightforward last lines. (Although it may be only my ignorance that makes them seem straightforward since Shackleton-Bailey finds their pertinence as obscure as Rosenblum?)

Even so, I think the tone of the poem essentially changes from vituperation to sex talk once you approach it as being addressed not to some third party, but to the "hermaphrodite" girl. But to do this, you have to abandon literal-mindedness and allow yourself to fall into Luxorius' "unpretentious play." This is, after all a poem not a polemic, and what's needed is to shift from the literal to the metaphoric.

> *Hermaphrodite Girl*

> *As if you were a double-organed*
> *monster-woman who, rather than joyfully*
> *stuffing herself*
> *when she gets excited*
> *can't help her compulsive erection.*

> *Why do you hide behind that frantic*
> *pretend pleasure? You never really*
> *give your cunt, neither open up nor squeeze.*

If you want to prove you're a grown up woman,
quit playing the role and be my girl.

I added the opening phrase "as if" and slightly softened *futui furente cunno*. Otherwise, the interpretation is, I think, reasonably unembellished. Rather than an example of decadence, I think *puellam hermaphroditam* may be an example of a sex poem territory discovered and claimed by Luxorious, a poem unlike anything before or after him. He was, to judge from his comments, politically incorrect in his own day. He's remained so, if for varying reasons, in every era since. But his ability to almost clinically examine the sexually grotesque image and find and caress the pleasure nerve seems unique.

Other titles from Otis Books | Seismicity Editions

Erik Anderson, *The Poetics of Trespass*
Published 2010 | 112 Pages | $12.95
ISBN-13: 978-0-979-6177-7-5
ISBN-10: 0-979-6166-7-4

J. Reuben Appelman, *Make Loneliness*
Published 2008 | 84 pages | $12.95
ISBN-13: 978-0-9796177-0-6
ISBN-10: 0-9796177-0-7

Bruce Bégout, *Common Place. The American Motel.*
Published 2010 | 143 Pages | $12.95
ISBN-13: 978-0-979-6177-8-2
ISBN-10: 0-979-6177-8-

Guy Bennett, *Self-Evident Poems*
Published 2011 | 96 pages | $12.95
ISBN-13: 978-0-9845289-0-5
ISBN-10: 0-9845289-0-3

Guy Bennett and Béatrice Mousli, Editors, *Seeing Los Angeles:
A Different Look at a Different City*
Published 2007 | 202 pages | $12.95
ISBN-13: 978-0-9755924-9-6
ISBN-10: 0-9755924-9-1

Robert Crosson, *Signs/ & Signals: The Daybooks of Robert Crosson*
Published 2008 | 245 Pages | $14.95
ISBN: 978-0-9796177-3-7

Robert Crosson, *Daybook (1983–86)*
Published 2011 | 96 Pages | $12.95
ISBN-13: 978-0-9845289-1-2
ISBN- 0-9845289-1-1

Ray DiPalma, *The Ancient Use of Stone:
Journals and Daybooks, 1998–2008*
Published 2009 | 216 pages | $14.95
ISBN: 978-0-9796177-5-1

Jean-Michel Espitallier, *Espitallier's Theorem*
Translated from the French by Guy Bennett
    Published 2003 | 137 pages | $12.95
    ISBN: 0-9755924-2-4

Leland Hickman, *Tiresias: The Collected Poems of Leland Hickman*
    Published 2009 | 205 Pages | $14.95
    ISBN: 978-0-9822645-1-5

Norman M. Klein, *Freud in Coney Island and Other Tales*
    Published 2006 | 104 pages | $12.95
    ISBN: 0-9755924-6-7

Ken McCullough, *Left Hand*
    Published 2004 | 191 pages | $12.95
    ISBN: 0-9755924-1-6

Béatrice Mousli, Editor, *Review of Two Worlds:*
French and American Poetry in Translation
    Published 2005 | 148 pages | $12.95
    ISBN: 0-9755924-3-2

Ryan Murphy, *Down with the Ship*
    Published 2006 | 66 pages | $12.95
    ISBN: 0-9755924-5-9

Dennis Phillips, *Navigation: Selected Poems, 1985–2010*
    Published 2011 | 288 pages | $14.95
    ISBN 13: 978-0-9845289-4-3
    ISBN: 0-9845289-4-6

Antonio Porta, *Piercing the Page: Selected Poems 1958–1989*
    Published 2011 | 368 pages | $14.95
    ISBN-13: 978-0-9845289-5-0
    ISBN: 0-9845289-5-4

Eric Priestley, *For Keeps*
    Published 2009 | 264 pages | $12.95
    ISBN: 978-0-979-6177-4-4

Ari Samsky, *The Capricious Critic*
  Published 2010 | 240 pages | $12.95
  ISBN-13: 978-0-979-177-6-8
  ISBN: 0-979-6177-6-6

Hélène Sanguinetti, *Hence This Cradle*
Translated from the French by Ann Cefola
  Published 2007 | 160 pages | $12.95
  ISBN: 970-0-9755924-7-2

Janet Sarbanes, *Army of One*
  Published 2008 | 173 pages | $12.95
  ISBN-13: 978-0-9796177-1-3
  ISBN-10: 0-9796177-1-5

Severo Sarduy, *Beach Birds*
Translated from the Spanish by Suzanne Jill Levine and Carol Maier
  Published 2007 | 182 pages | $12.95
  ISBN: 978-9755924-8-9

Adriano Spatola, *The Porthole*
Translated from the Italian by Beppe Cavatorta and Polly Geller
  Published 2011 | 112 pages | $12.95
  ISBN 13: 978-0-9796177-9-9
  ISBN-10: 0-9796177-9-0

Adriano Spatola, *Toward Total Poetry*
Translated from the Italian by Brendan W. Hennessey and Guy Bennett
with an Introduction by Guy Bennett
  Published 2008 | 176 pages | $12.95
  ISBN 13: 978-0-9796177-2-0
  ISBN-10: 0-9796177-3-1

Carol Treadwell, *Spots and Trouble Spots*
  Published 2004 | 176 pages | $12.95
  ISBN: 0-9755924-0-8

Allyssa Wolf, *Vaudeville*
  Published 2006 | 82 pages | $12.95
  ISBN: 0-9755924-4-0